Overcoming IT Complexity

Simplify Operations, Enable Innovation,
and Cultivate Successful Cloud Outcomes

Lee Atchison

Beijing · Boston · Farnham · Sebastopol · Tokyo

Overcoming IT Complexity

by Lee Atchison

Published by O'Reilly Media, Inc., 1005 Gravenstein Highway North, Sebastopol, CA 95472.

O'Reilly books may be purchased for educational, business, or sales promotional use. Online editions are also available for most titles (*http://oreilly.com*). For more information, contact our corporate/institutional sales department: 800-998-9938 or *corporate@oreilly.com*.

Acquisitions Editor: Megan Laddusaw	**Indexer:** nSight, Inc.
Development Editor: Gary O'Brien	**Interior Designer:** Monica Kamsvaag
Production Editor: Beth Kelly	**Cover Designer:** Susan Thompson
Copyeditor: Rachel Head	**Illustrator:** Kate Dullea
Proofreader: Audrey Doyle	

December 2022:   First Edition

Revision History for the First Edition

2022-12-09:   First Release

See *http://oreilly.com/catalog/errata.csp?isbn=9781492098492* for release details.

978-1-492-09850-8

[LSI]

To Beth

My love, my life, my everything

Contents

| Foreword | vii |

| Preface | xi |

1 | What Is the Modern IT Complexity Dilemma? | 1 |

2 | Auditing and Assessing Your IT Ecosystem | 25 |

3 | Moving to an Adaptive Architecture | 41 |

4 | Managing Knowledge | 57 |

5 | Creating Your Technology Investment Framework | 75 |

6 | Starting the Conversation | 85 |

| Index | 89 |

Foreword

I have spent my career developing and operating software and modernizing product and engineering teams, from startups to large enterprises. I founded Interland (now Web.com) in my 20s and went on to drive transformation at scale while leading development and operations at Cox Automotive, Unqork, and New Relic. I have been a CEO, CTO, and CPO and have worked to help other enterprises around the globe transform. I have also been an author and speaker on topics including DevOps, digital transformation, Agile, Scrum, and Lean Startup. My experience has given me a unique perspective on how the internet has narrowed competitive moats and forced every company to learn how to operate like a digital business—not just say they are one.

It is my pleasure to write this foreword for Lee's new book, *Overcoming IT Complexity*. Like his previous book, *Architecting for Scale* (O'Reilly), I believe this will become the reference guide for overcoming the diverse difficulties companies face—whether they are SaaS, non-SaaS, or non-technology-focused IT firms. As Lee explains in this book, one of the many challenges companies face while trying to deliver new features and functionality in order to stay competitive is quickly accumulating technical debt. With a cutting-edge approach, including enterprise risk management and strategies for measuring results, Lee lays out a comprehensive framework for dealing with that technical debt.

The Growing Complexity of IT Environments

Technology has grown increasingly complex over the years, but the rate of its evolution has increased dramatically in the last decade. Many factors are driving this fast evolution:

- The rising number of devices connecting to the internet, from laptops and smartphones to smart home products
- The increase in cloud services
- The expansion in the number of devices that can be connected to create a single application
- The development of artificial intelligence and machine learning, which has led to innovative new products that help automate traditional business processes
- The evolution of open source software, which has made it easier for developers to create innovative new products

The numerous applications and devices employees use across an organization's environment generate fragmentation. This fragmentation is a big challenge for the IT department, and it can be hard to detect because it may be distributed across various systems your organization uses (sometimes without employees knowing about it):

- Applications can be fragmented across numerous databases, including cloud databases.
- Virtual machines (VMs) are often fragmented across multiple servers.
- Physical servers are often fragmented across multiple physical locations.
- Network infrastructure and cloud services can also become fragmented.

Complexity can increase the time it takes to deliver new IT solutions or roll out new services. It can also slow down processes such as equipment procurement and software upgrades. Complexity can be particularly problematic for business users, who may have limited knowledge of the technologies used by their organization's IT department. This can make it difficult for these users to collaborate with the IT department on projects or get the kind of support they need when issues arise. It can also make it difficult for the IT department to keep track of everything being used across the organization and ensure that it's all secure.

The complexity of building API-first and embedded SaaS solutions is rising as new applications are based on open source platforms. Every day, delivering new value while satisfying customers becomes more difficult. Even if your IT organization is still struggling to eradicate the Node.js monolith or is striving to scale to billions of transactions, Lee provides ideas based on Adaptive Architecture principles and the crucial elements of flexible infrastructure as code to help you reduce technical debt and IT complexity.

—Ken Gavranovic
CEO of AGS LLC;
Former CEO of Web.com
(Interland), GM of Product and
Engineering at New Relic,
and VP of Digital Systems
at COX Automotive

Preface

The complexity of modern IT systems can impact your application's quality and security.

It's that simple.

Business pressures have caused IT organizations to focus on creating new applications and adding new features and capabilities to existing applications to meet increasing competitive demands. The result is insufficient time to work on managing, operating, and maintaining existing applications and capabilities. Ignoring ongoing issues increases technical debt, which in turn increases the complexity of modern systems. Increased system complexity makes adding new features and capabilities harder, and the vicious circle continues.

Addressing the IT complexity dilemma is essential, but it is not easy. In this book, we begin by examining this dilemma and how it impacts you, your applications, and your organization. Then we talk about identifying and measuring complexity in your organization today. How can you measure complexity without introducing complex measurement systems? Since you can't improve a system until you can measure it, this ability is critical to managing IT complexity.

Next, we examine solutions for reducing IT complexity and the cognitive load it induces. We discuss the role of adaptive architectures in modernizing applications, considering both how they can reduce complexity and the risk of increased complexity they may carry.

We then explore how knowledge management techniques can assist in reducing cognitive load and IT complexity, and how your strategy for investing in your infrastructure impacts complexity.

Finally, I provide some advice on how to begin conversations within your organization about the impact of IT complexity on your company, your products, and your applications.

The goal of this book is to give you the tools you need to understand how IT complexity can negatively impact your company and your applications, and how you can break the cycle to effectively manage its effect on your organization.

More Information

This book is just a starting point in your journey to managing your IT systems and experiences. If you want to learn more, feel free to check out the other books, articles, courses, and interviews by the author at *leeatchison.com*. Also, check out the other great books and online courses O'Reilly Media offers.

O'Reilly Online Learning

O'REILLY® For more than 40 years, *O'Reilly Media* has provided technology and business training, knowledge, and insight to help companies succeed.

Our unique network of experts and innovators share their knowledge and expertise through books, articles, and our online learning platform. O'Reilly's online learning platform gives you on-demand access to live training courses, in-depth learning paths, interactive coding environments, and a vast collection of text and video from O'Reilly and 200+ other publishers. For more information, visit *https://oreilly.com*.

How to Contact Us

Please address comments and questions concerning this book to the publisher:

O'Reilly Media, Inc.

1005 Gravenstein Highway North

Sebastopol, CA 95472

800-998-9938 (in the United States or Canada)

707-829-0515 (international or local)

707-829-0104 (fax)

We have a web page for this book, where we list errata, examples, and any additional information. You can access this page at *https://oreil.ly/overcoming-it-complexity*.

Email *bookquestions@oreilly.com* to comment or ask technical questions about this book.

Visit *https://oreilly.com* for more information and news about our books and courses.

Find us on LinkedIn: *https://linkedin.com/company/oreilly-media*

Follow us on Twitter: *https://twitter.com/oreillymedia*

Watch us on YouTube: *https://youtube.com/oreillymedia*

Acknowledgments

While there are more people who helped make this book possible than I could possibly ever list here, I do want to mention several people who were particularly helpful to me.

Ken Gavranovic. The word *friend* is an understatement. My *virtual brother* is more descriptive. Ken, always trust the power of monkeys.

Kurt Kufeld, Greg Hart, Scott Green, Patrick Franklin, Suresh Kumar, Colin Bodell, Adam Selipsky, and Andy Jassy. You gave me opportunities at Amazon and AWS I could not have ever imagined.

Bjorn Freeman-Benson, Kevin McGuire, Abner Germanow, Darren Cunningham, Jay Fry, Bharath Gowda. Each of these people, in their own way, contributed significantly to my growing career at New Relic, and ultimately to my ability to work as an independent consultant, author, advisor, and thought leader.

Robson Grieve. Besides giving me huge opportunities at New Relic, he hired me as a consultant when I first put out my shingle—he was literally my first customer. He believed in me. In fact, he believed in me twice.

Jennifer Pollock, my longtime O'Reilly acquisitions editor (recently promoted to senior content director), Megan Laddusaw, my current O'Reilly acquisitions editor, and Gary O'Brien, my development editor for this book. Jennifer, congratulations on your promotion—I always love working with you on projects. Megan, I look forward to many years working with you. Gary, you've been a great partner, helping bring this book together.

And finally, and perhaps most significantly, I'd like to thank Mark Menger from F5. Mark spent many hours with me talking through the topics I discuss in this book. His insights were invaluable. Without him, this book would not have happened.

What Is the Modern IT Complexity Dilemma?

The complexity of modern IT systems supporting modern applications can impact your customers, your partners, your employees, and the quality and security of your application. And the simple act of maintaining, growing, and maturing IT systems inevitably makes them more complex.

The *IT complexity dilemma* refers to the challenges businesses face when trying to manage and optimize their IT operations. The increasing complexity of modern IT systems has made it difficult for businesses to keep up with technology changes and make necessary updates to their infrastructure, in turn making it difficult for them to realize their desired return on their technology investments. Business pressures have caused IT organizations to focus increasingly on creating new features and focus less on resolving ongoing problems and upgrading existing architectures. This has led to a buildup of technical debt, which can have consequences such as slowed business processes, increased IT costs, and even system failures. Addressing this complexity dilemma is essential, but it is not easy.

There are several measures that businesses can take to mitigate the effects of the IT complexity dilemma, including investing in automation technologies, establishing standard operating procedures, and hiring skilled IT professionals. By taking these steps, businesses can improve their ability to manage and optimize their IT operations, minimizing the negative impacts of complexity.

However, even with these measures in place, businesses will still face challenges in managing their IT operations due to the growing complexity of modern IT systems. By attempting to mitigate the effects of this complexity, businesses can improve their efficiency, security, and competitiveness in today's IT environment.

As we will discuss later in this chapter, technical debt is at the core of the complexity dilemma: indeed, technical debt and complexity go hand in hand. And as you will see, dealing effectively with technical debt involves much more than just refactoring code.

Technical debt and complexity go hand in hand.

Technical debt is a metric that describes everything that interferes with an application's smooth operation and customer experience. In other words, it is everything that makes the application complex or fragile, thereby contributing to operational complexity, complicating customer experiences, or simply making the application more difficult to enhance, expand, and improve.

But before we can talk about ways to reduce complexity, it's important to understand how IT organizations are structured in modern enterprises, and how the operations and development teams within the IT organization interact to create a working system.

The Structure of Modern IT Organizations

IT organizations vary considerably in size and shape. A modern IT organization uses DevOps methodologies. The organization is typically a relatively flat, matrix-type structure in which teams of developers and operators work together closely. To keep up with the fast pace of customer demand and technological change, both teams need to adapt quickly. The development team needs to be able to build new systems and applications and repair and upgrade existing systems quickly. The operations team must be able to not only deploy and manage those systems rapidly but also detect and resolve problems when they occur. A close working relationship between development and operations is critical to maintaining this speed.

However, natural separations start taking shape as applications grow in complexity and the organization grows in size. Traditional divisions between development and operations begin to formalize, and the space between the two groups expands.

In the past, a flat management structure has been able to assist the organization in keeping the communications channels flowing, encouraging dialog among the development, operations, security, and product leadership teams. But as the organization grows, keeping the management structure flat and responsive becomes harder and harder.

Management and organizational structures are required to keep the growing organization operational. Formalized processes help yield consistent results and plans. Yet, these same structures and processes create a natural blockage to communication flow. This

Ironically, the biggest inhibitor to growth is, in fact, growth.

blockage makes it harder for the organization to function. Teams split, and organizational distancing limits cooperation and communication. This limits growth.

Ironically, the biggest inhibitor to growth is, in fact, growth. The organizational structure gets more complex, and the application gets more complex.

Since an IT organization is only as good as the management that drives it, it is essential to have a strong and effective management team in place. This team is responsible for steering the organization in the right direction, setting goals and objectives, and ensuring that all aspects are running smoothly.

The management team must also adapt to changes quickly and respond to new market demands effectively. They must work across organizational boundaries, and operate in unison with all product, development, operational, and support teams.

How the IT organization is structured varies considerably based on the nature of the business. The type of company (software focused, SaaS focused, nonsoftware focused, etc.) is the biggest indicator of the structure of the IT organization.

THE ROLE OF SOFTWARE DEVELOPMENT IN IT ORGANIZATIONS

Within an IT organization, the structure and responsibility of the development team is related to the nature of the business and the structure of the rest of the company. The development team may have a limited role in managing internal processes and systems, or it may be an integral part of the company's core business model. This means there is no one-size-fits-all organizational structure that defines a modern IT organization.

But we can generalize. For this discussion, we're going to define three types of businesses:

1. Nonsoftware-focused IT organizations

2. Non-Software-as-a-Service (SaaS) software-focused IT organizations

3. SaaS-focused IT organizations

In the following sections, we will explore the characteristics of each type of company and the IT organization, structure that tends to occur in each.

In practice, you will likely find that your circumstances lead to an amalgam of two or three of these types.

Business type 1: The nonsoftware-focused IT organization

Type 1 is a business with a primary purpose other than producing, selling, or operating software. This includes nearly all nontechnology-focused companies, such as banks, restaurants, stores, taxi services, airlines, railroads, media companies, etc. The mission of a nonsoftware company is not technology focused. It may use software as a tool internally to manage sales, marketing, manufacturing, or other business processes, but software is secondary to its primary business.

As such, there are no large application development teams. There is an IT organization, and within that are relatively small (compared to the overall size of the company) development and operations teams, but only a small portion of the company's resources are invested in IT systems and personnel.

Figure 1-1 illustrates this. The company leadership has bigger things to focus on, leaving IT leadership to manage these small development and operations teams.

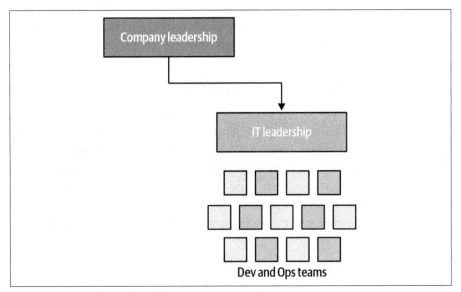

Figure 1-1. A nonsoftware-focused company

For these more traditional nonsoftware-based enterprise companies, the IT organization has a purely supportive role. It is primarily operations focused, though it may also have some development capabilities. Tooling and operational processes are the central areas of concern.

Business type 2: The non-SaaS software IT organization

The primary purpose of the second type of business is creating software that it sells to other people or companies. It typically does not operate the software for its customers; instead, the software (which does not require a significant backend SaaS-like application to function) is operated directly by the customer.

Examples of this type of software include popular workplace applications such as Microsoft Word and Adobe Illustrator, as well as games (such as *Angry Birds*), music applications, and ebook readers. It may also include tools like antivirus software, firewalls, and news aggregators.

A non-SaaS software organization has a software- or engineering-focused mission. These organizations have high-caliber application development teams, but typically do not have a strong operations team. Because the software they produce is operated by customers, not by the company itself, there is no need for a large operational focus.

A generic IT organization provides tools and processes that support the company as a whole. Part of its role is to provide support for the product development teams (as well as sales/marketing, etc.), but it does not directly contribute to product development or operations. Figure 1-2 shows this structure.

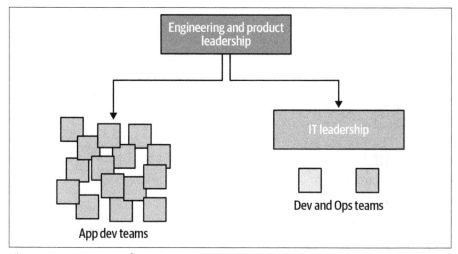

Figure 1-2. A non-SaaS software company

Non-SaaS software companies have a strong focus on application development teams, but these are not DevOps teams; they are independent software development teams that produce software that is sold and delivered to customers. The IT organization is small and supports the company as a whole, including the development and operation of tools for internal use; it is separate and isolated from the product development teams.

Business type 3: The SaaS-focused IT organization

The third type of business is a company whose primary purpose is to create a SaaS application or to operate customer software. This includes business-to-business (B2B) companies providing services such as inventory management, financial planning, communications, and sales infrastructure. Examples of SaaS products and companies include Intuit QuickBooks, Slack, Shopify, Mailchimp, and Salesforce.

There are also business-to-consumer (B2C) SaaS companies providing entertainment, retail shopping, and social media services. Examples of B2C SaaS companies include Amazon (retail), Netflix, Facebook, and Twitter.

A highly functional SaaS organization requires a high-caliber application development team *and* a high-caliber operations team. The two teams must cooperate to succeed. Figure 1-3 shows the typical organizational structure.

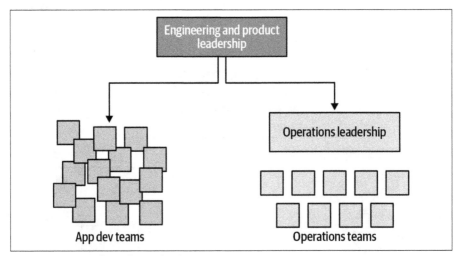

Figure 1-3. A SaaS-focused organization

The application development teams in a SaaS company are typically proportionately large groups that require substantial investments in engineering and product management. Each team owns a part of the overall SaaS application and builds, tests, deploys, operates, and maintains only the services it is responsible for. Operations teams provide a smooth operations infrastructure that supports the development teams. The enterprise's focus is typically primarily on the software development teams. These companies may have separate IT organizations to support business processes, but the application development teams are not part of that organization.

In these high-tech, software-driven companies, the application development teams are a core component of the enterprise. Given its importance, this group reports high in the company's organizational hierarchy.

Notice that some companies fit into multiple categories. For instance, Microsoft offers SaaS services (Office 365) and non-SaaS software (Microsoft Word and Halo). Amazon offers B2C services (Amazon retail) and B2B services (AWS), along with non-SaaS services (Kindle readers). Additionally, a company like Charles Schwab may offer investment software as a service, yet also focus on general financial services and investments. These enterprises may have different divisions that appear to be separate companies, each structured differently, or they may have a hybrid structure. Keep in mind that the categories discussed here are generalizations.

DEVELOPMENT AND OPERATIONS IN THE IT ORGANIZATION

Within an IT organization, the development and operations teams are focused on driving the tooling and resources needed to operate the company, including building applications necessary for the company to run. The responsibilities of these teams and the processes they follow depend on where the company fits within the three types of organizations we just discussed, as do the types of talent they attract.

Development

There is a direct correlation between the amount of *focus your company places on software development* and the *availability of high-quality technical talent* and software leadership available to your organization. The best software developers, architects, and software leaders tend to gravitate toward the much more lucrative opportunities in SaaS application development and other software-centric companies.

This means that organizations in which software plays only a secondary role in the mission find it difficult to attract and retain software talent. Often this means the organization as a whole suffers. Yes, there are high-quality, talented developers in these organizations, but they are much harder to locate and hire. This tends to result in there being less innovation and fewer creative solutions to problems in these types of organizations. Rather than being state-of-the-art, the software applications created in such organizations tend to be fairly prosaic, supportive applications.

The caliber of your IT development team is critically important in determining the sophistication of the applications your organization can support, and your organization's ability to respond to the inevitable increase in complexity that occurs over time.

The result is that organizations in which software is a secondary part of the business rather than the primary focus tend to be more sensitive to the IT complexity dilemma.

Operations

Operations teams, on the other hand, tend to attract high-quality talent based on how central the organization's operational aspects are to the business focus. This means SaaS companies, which are highly dependent on high-quality operations teams, tend to attract higher-quality operational talent than organizations in which operations are secondary to the goals of the business.

Less attractive o operational talent are nonsoftware companies that require a significant internal software infrastructure to keep the organization running smoothly. This includes organizations such as banks and other financial firms where the software infrastructure is critically important and must stay operational.

Even less attractive to operational talent are companies that produce "boxed" software that is operated on customer computers and systems, rather than in internal operational environments.

This makes sense. SaaS companies rely heavily on highly performant operational environments and invest heavily in these areas. This investment, and the opportunities it produces, attracts top operational engineering talent to these organizations. Organizations that are less operations focused need less investment in this area, and hence don't attract as much interest.

The traditional operational landscape is changing, however. Many traditional operational capabilities are now handled by outsourced infrastructure, such as

SaaS applications and cloud service providers. Additionally, newer tooling and capabilities automate a large portion of basic operational requirements.

Infrastructure as Code (IaC) and *Operations as Code* (OaC) tools help with this effort, and strive to make operational setup and basic operational responsibilities automated and repeatable. This improves overall operational reliability. Additionally, since scripts and script-like descriptions drive IaC and OaC, these capabilities encourage code as documentation and knowledge sharing of the operational environments involved. Finally, since IaC and OaC generalize the operational aspects of an application into code-like capabilities, they allow the use of standardized and well-understood development processes, such as revision management. Revision management allows tracking and correlating failures to changes, reducing mistakes, increasing security and traceability, and improving overall accountability and performance.

The role of DevOps in the modernization of the enterprise

DevOps is a term in wide use in modern organizations. It describes, in part, the collaboration between development and operations teams within an organization. The intent of DevOps is to break down the traditional barriers that exist between these two groups and encourage collaboration and cooperation, allowing them to work together more effectively and efficiently. This leads to faster problem solving, increased efficiency and responsiveness, and overall higher application quality and availability. DevOps is becoming the norm in modern IT organizations.

In a DevOps organization, individual teams each own some portion of the application. In modern applications, these components are typically services. The individual teams are responsible for the development, testing, deployment, operation, and ongoing support of the services assigned to their care.

Figure 1-4 shows the organizational structure at a software company that uses DevOps principles. As such, it describes the same sort of SaaS company described back in Figure 1-3. The primary difference is that both the development aspects and most of the operational aspects of ownership are assigned to the same team under the engineering and product leadership organization. There is still a very thin operations support organization, but the job of this organization is not to manage the operations of the application; rather, its role is to provide tools and assistance to the product teams that own and operate the individual services.

Merging the responsibility for the development and operations of individual services into a single organization in this way lowers the communication barriers that typically existed in the past between the development and operations teams, improving the organization's overall performance and reliability.

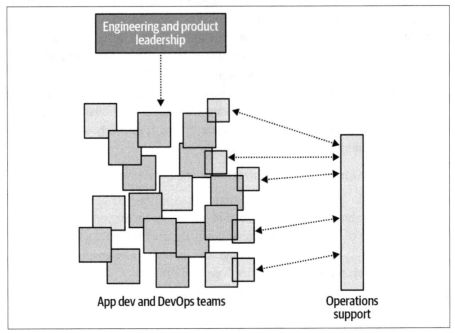

Figure 1-4. A DevOps-focused software company

Now that we understand more about how modern IT organizations are structured, we can talk about the problem complexity poses in these organizations and how complexity impacts the long-term viability and success of the organization.

The Advent of Complexity

It's hard to pinpoint exactly when complexity begins to creep in within a young IT organization, but it's usually tied to some decision that is meant to reduce time to market or cost to market, at the expense of some further work or cost later on. This kick starts the slow and inexorable growth in complexity. For larger, more established enterprises, introducing complexity is typically tied to incorporating technology into the established processes. In either case, the increase in complexity is linked to an increase in technical debt.

TECHNICAL DEBT: THE KEY TO COMPLEXITY

In software development, technical debt is the cost of additional rework caused by choosing an easy, limited, or suboptimal solution now, rather than using a better approach that would take longer or cost more money to implement up front.

Ward Cunningham originally coined the term. According to Ward, "technical debt includes those internal things that you choose not to do now, but which impede future development if left undone."

The code development aspect of technical debt only captures a small part of it. Technical debt applies to all aspects of modern application design, development, and long-term operation.

For SaaS and other cloud-centric applications, the long-term operational impact is a significant driver of technical debt. The longer an application operates, the greater the technical debt, and the greater an application's technical debt, the greater the negative impact on the long-term operation of the service.

When a development team at a SaaS company decides to add a new capability to an application but takes shortcuts in the architecture to launch the capability more quickly, it is adding to the technical debt of the application and the company as a whole. Unless a concerted effort is made to resolve the technical debt by completing the proper design and architecture, it will accumulate until it hinders development and operational processes.

Technical debt is similar to financial debt. In moderation, it can be handled and the cost can be dealt with. But if technical debt is not repaid, it can accrue "interest" in the form of additional technical debt—and just as with financial debt, if you accrue too much interest, you can no longer afford to repay the debt. Too much technical debt makes the changes necessary to resolve (or pay back) the technical debt harder and more expensive to implement.

Let your financial debt grow too large, and you will go broke. Let your technical debt grow too large, and your application will become unsupportable, unsustainable, and unmaintainable.

How does technical debt grow?

Technical debt can grow naturally and quietly during the normal product development process. Every project that contributes to a product also contributes to its technical debt—even adding a simple feature enhancement. This is illustrated at the top of Figure 1-5: during normal product development, work and outputs are added to the product, and some amount of debt is added to the stack of technical debt.

Sometimes, a project is done in a "quick and dirty" manner, such as when a new feature is added without proper design in order to get it out the door quickly. In these cases, the project adds more debt. Sometimes, the project can even add more technical debt to your application than the amount of real value it provides. This is the case with the example project shown in the middle of Figure 1-5.

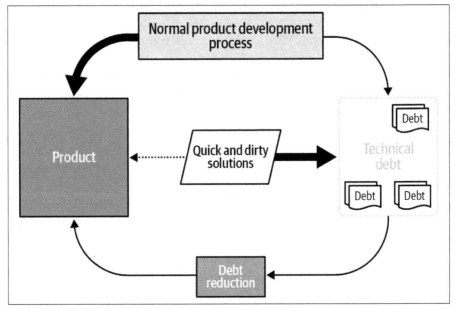

Figure 1-5. The flow of technical debt during product development

To keep technical debt from growing without bounds, some effort needs to be added to each project to reduce the technical debt. Keeping your technical debt at a sustainable level requires constant investment in reducing the technical debt over time.

This constant flow of increasing and decreasing technical debt is one of the reasons why it can sneak up on a product. If more debt is regularly added than is reduced from the backlog, the debt will grow, yet the growth may not be noticeable. It's not until the debt has grown to a point where it starts having a negative impact on your product that you will notice how much has accumulated. At this point, it may be too large to deal with effectively and easily.

Each project can either increase or decrease the technical debt within a system. In a full, high-quality project, the planned work often includes doing all the work necessary, along with working on reducing some amount of related technical debt. When the work is completed, the application's technical debt is lower than before. This is illustrated in Figure 1-6: the *work completed* for the project is larger than the project itself, and the extra effort is put toward reducing the size of the technical debt. This is a project that's dealing with technical debt in a healthy way.

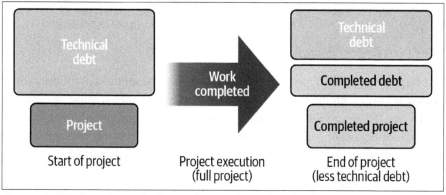

Figure 1-6. A full/complete project has to plan to reduce technical debt

Unfortunately, many projects are much more quick and dirty. They are designed to only complete as much work as is absolutely necessary, leaving the rest to be completed later. In fact, a common project management philosophy involves building a *minimum viable product*, or MVP—an approach that essentially dictates that you do as little product work as possible to get a functional product out the door.

The result is work that is not completed. More often than not, this increases the overall technical debt of the application. This phenomenon is illustrated in Figure 1-7. Here, the *work completed* is only part of that required by the project, and it is accompanied by an equal amount of *work not done*. This additional important work which was not completed ends up increasing the overall technical debt in the project.

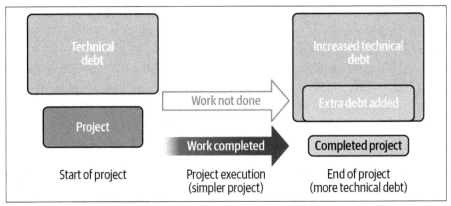

Figure 1-7. A quick and dirty project often increases technical debt

Depending on the types of projects undertaken, the amount of technical debt associated with a product will vary over time, sometimes decreasing, sometimes increasing. The more full, high-quality projects that are completed, the lower the overall technical debt will be. The more quick and dirty projects that are used to implement functionality, the higher the resulting technical debt will be.

The negative impact of technical debt

Sometimes, deciding to build a simpler solution now and delaying a longer-term implementation (as depicted in Figure 1-7) is advantageous. It allows you to get a solution out to customers earlier, so the company can start monetizing the change and receive customer input on what they like and do not like, which can be fed into a later, more ambitious solution. This is analogous to the idea that borrowing money is advantageous if you use the money to contribute to a greater cause, such as purchasing a home; paying some interest on borrowed money is fine, as long as the money you borrowed is put to good use. Similarly, managing some technical debt is useful and appropriate as long as the project that generates that debt adds value to your product and your company. Technical debt, like financial debt, becomes a problem when left unresolved: it increases in cost and gets harder to deal with over time.

Continuing with the financial metaphor, technical debt becomes a problem when it builds up to the point where the cost of managing and servicing the debt becomes too great and impedes your ability to invest in future projects. When too many quick and dirty projects rule your project plan, and projects designed to reduce debt are not staffed in your company, your technical debt starts to become unmanageable. If this goes on for too long, technical debt overwhelms the project, as shown in Figure 1-8.

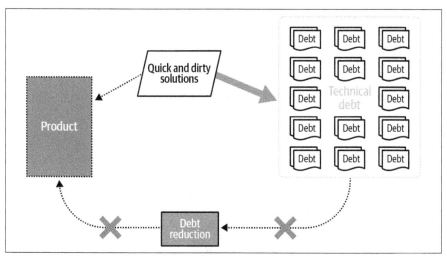

Figure 1-8. Technical debt overwhelming the project

In this scenario, servicing the debt becomes the dominant role of your team, and you spend little or no time contributing to improving the product. Your debt is too large to be effectively managed, and the product suffers.

THE ORGANIZATIONAL PAIN OF COMPLEXITY

Technical debt and complexity go hand in hand. So do complexity and organizational pain. While technical debt is not a complete picture of application complexity, the growth of technical debt is tied very closely to the growth of application complexity.

As your application gets more and more complex, many things happen to it:

It becomes brittle.

A complex application is subject to minor issues quickly escalating into major problems. While most applications operate in a well of a positive feedback cycle, a complex application's operational well turns into a negative feedback cycle, where it's difficult to deal with even small problems. As Figure 1-9 shows, a stable application tends to stay in the valley between the two hills representing application failure, building success upon success, while a brittle application is ready to roll off the top of the hill into failure at the smallest of nudges.

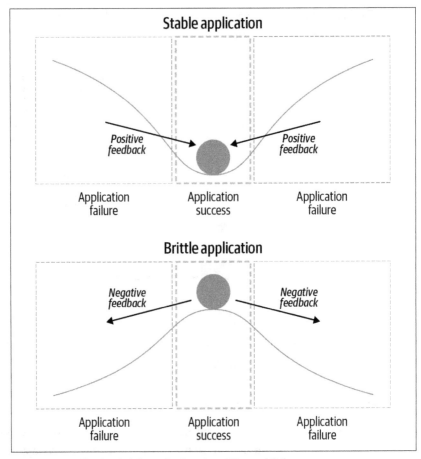

Figure 1-9. Application brittleness leads to instability and failure

Fewer engineers have complete knowledge of the application.

Only the most senior engineers, those who have been working on the application the longest, have a broad understanding of how the complete application works. As time goes on, their knowledge becomes diluted: it may be less accurate, higher level, or more specialized. As an application grows in complexity, maintaining detailed knowledge of the application as a whole is no longer possible for single individuals.

The knowledge that engineers do have about the application becomes obsolete more quickly.

Complex applications change frequently, and engineers' knowledge about how the application works quickly becomes outdated.

It gets harder to bring new engineers up to speed.

Complex applications have long learning paths. This is not only because there is more to learn, but also because the knowledge new engineers need to become productive is more distributed, and often anecdotal and out of date.

The net result of these issues is higher organizational pain. This pain translates into poor-quality changes, less-motivated staff, and, ultimately, staff turnover. Higher turnover means an additional need to recruit and train new engineers, which gets harder as the pain increases. Brittleness leads to lower availability, and customer-visible issues and failures.

Messy desk syndrome

Imagine you have a perfectly clean desk. Now, take a sheet of paper and set it in the corner. Is your desk messy? No, not yet. Now take 50 other related sheets of paper and sit them on top of the one sheet in the corner. Is your desk messy? No, not yet. Now imagine you have more papers, but these don't go with the stack in the corner; they are for different projects. So you put them in different locations on the desk that seem to make sense, just single sheets in single locations. Then, over time, you put more papers and documents and books and folders and pictures, one at a time, on the desk. If you don't know where something goes, you just put it in a new location. You'll figure it out later. Now your desk is messy. In fact, it's extremely messy.

This happened because you didn't have a plan from the beginning, and decided to just "wing it" along the way. You made your desk messy simply by using and working on it. The moral of the story? Unless you have a solid plan for organizing the papers on your desk established *at the beginning*, and you stick with it, sooner or later your desk will become messy, one sheet at a time.

The same thing happens with organizational pain: it grows quickly when you don't have an architectural plan from the beginning and you take things as they come. You "wing it," metaphorically speaking. The result is that you add to your technical debt, and hence your organizational pain, simply by working on and building the application.

Every action you take contributes to that organizational pain, little by little. Your technical debt grows a bit at a time until it becomes overwhelming.

Let's change our login process to allow saving login credentials in the user's browser.

Let's add this new feature to that menu.

Users would prefer that this feature works in three steps rather than the current four steps. Let's combine two of the steps.

We need to remove the per-session limit on this resource.

We don't have time to build this full feature now, but we can build this smaller feature, which will make many customers happier. We can do the rest later.

Let's release this feature this way first, and then we can collect input from customers and modify it to make it more user friendly as we get more input.

Any one of these statements could correspond to a simple set of changes that makes perfect sense at the time. It might not have any obvious impact on overall technical debt at all.

But the little changes...and the little debt...and the little impact...they add up, like the little pieces of paper and other items on your desk. As with the desk that starts clean and ends up messy, each action you take may, individually, seem perfectly benign. Those actions may look perfectly acceptable. But over time, as a whole, they become overwhelming.

Icing the Cake

Many IT organizations use the expression "icing the cake." This is when you describe the current situation as "everything is OK," whether it actually is OK or not.

The slow accrual of technical debt and organizational pain leads to this process of icing the cake. At the start, all is well and it's easy to say "everything is OK," because it is—or at least it appears to be.

But as time goes on, and technical debt increases, and organizational pain increases, little by little, things aren't OK anymore. Still, the tendency to keep saying "everything is OK" is strong. The organization keeps icing the cake.

The problem is that a pain-ridden organization working on a debt-ridden application and still saying that "everything is OK" is simply failing to notice or accept what's obvious to every outsider—the pain is real, and the organization is not OK. Without anyone noticing it, the icing went bad.

COMPLEXITY IN AN IT ORGANIZATION

Complexity grows in IT organizations as well. First, it creeps into your application. As your application grows more complex, so does the infrastructure needed to run the application. So your IT operations become more complex. And your engineering organization becomes more complex. Thus, *managing* your IT gets more complex.

> *As complexity increases, the ability of the organization to change direction quickly and respond to new demands diminishes.*

What started as a simple change in the needs of your application balloons into the growth of a complex IT organization.

As complexity increases, the ability of the organization to change direction quickly and respond to new demands diminishes. A once-agile organization becomes less agile.

Over time, an agile organization thus evolves into either a rigid organization—one that fears and rejects change, in an effort to keep the system stable and supported—or a fragile organization, where every minor change risks breaking a larger system or process, limiting the ability to adjust and grow. This is illustrated in Figure 1-10.

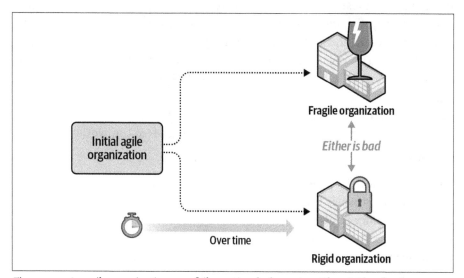

Figure 1-10. An agile organization may fail over time by becoming either rigid or fragile

Almost independent of the specific company, complexity and technical debt correspond to a lowered ability to respond to market and competitive demands.

Why is this true? There are typically two reasons why application complexity leads a company to lower agility.

First, when an organization has overly complex applications, changes to those applications are increasingly likely to cause problems. Small changes and small adjustments cause large failures and outages to occur. This makes the organization hesitate. Changes go through additional review cycles, changes get consolidated, changes that don't show clear value are discarded as too dangerous. Rather than having a "Yes, we can try that!" attitude, the organization adopts a much more conservative view. "No, not unless it's absolutely necessary" becomes the more likely position.

This reaction is intended to keep the application from failing. It's the company's response to keeping the application robust—the fewer changes you make, the safer the application is.

As a result, the application development process slows down considerably. This makes the application—and the company—significantly less agile than its competitors.

Second, if the organization doesn't naturally slow down and continues to make changes, those changes become increasingly risky. Because of the application complexity, the organization may make changes without fully understanding what's involved in them. This leads to dangerous changes, and these changes break things. The organization doesn't slow down and become conservative, but instead moves forward recklessly. The result? Application availability suffers and customer issues increase. Technical debt also increases, feeding into the complexity and creating a vicious circle. Complexity leads to brittleness which leads to failures which lead to technical debt which leads to complexity.

IT DEATH

So technical debt leads to complexity, and complexity leads to organizational pain. This all ultimately leads to *IT death.*

But what does IT death look like?

IT death is what happens to an organization when the pain of complexity sends the organization into a state of ineffectualness. It cannot improve, it cannot grow, and hence it stagnates. Since its competitors will continue to grow, an organization's stagnation ultimately leads to its death.

There are many examples of where this has happened.

Xerox, long the leader in producing photocopiers for large organizations, suffered from an inability to pivot from copiers to the personal computer (PC). Despite the fact that the modern PC user interface was originally conceived at Xerox's Palo Alto Research Center (PARC), the company was unable to compete with Microsoft and Apple in developing a PC operating system. Arguably, without Xerox PARC, there would be no Apple Macintosh computer, yet Xerox's inability to pivot kept it from capitalizing on this innovation.

And it's not just technology companies that suffer this fate. Firestone, the tire company, was facing the difficult task of modernizing its tire creation process in light of radial tire technology created by one of its competitors, Michelin. Firestone bogged down and could not update its processes to handle the new technology. Try as it might, it kept making tires that customers did not want, and its business suffered. Ultimately, Firestone was absorbed by Bridgestone. This is an example of what *Harvard Business Review* calls *active inertia* (*https://oreil.ly/HUbjr*).

Many other highly innovative companies have fallen into the trap of IT death by losing their ability to innovate. Hewlett-Packard, one of the founding companies of Silicon Valley—the heart of technical innovation across the world—experienced this problem, falling into a slow death spiral.

Polaroid suffered a similar fate when it failed to innovate new camera technology, as did Blockbuster Video, which failed to recognize the importance of video streaming technology, and the bookstore Borders, which was overwhelmed by the innovation of upstart Amazon.com.

Technical debt and complexity slow down innovation. They keep companies from staying competitive, which ultimately results in their eventual downfall, and potentially even death.

WHAT MAKES A MATURE IT ORGANIZATION

A mature IT organization is agile. It can make decisions quickly and easily, stick by those decisions until organizational needs dictate a change, and implement them quickly and effectively.

Why is it important for a mature IT organization to be agile? When agility is hampered, companies fall into two traps that can bring them down:

- Lack of competitive offerings
- Unsafe security vulnerabilities

Let's look at each of these more closely.

Competitive offerings

Maintaining competitiveness is critical to a modern application. This is because the pace of change is accelerating. Technology is advancing rapidly, and new competitors are constantly emerging. Your competitors are moving faster than ever before, and if you can't keep pace with them you will quickly fall behind and soon become irrelevant. Keeping pace means moving faster and faster, which means being able to adapt and change as the situation demands.

Customers are constantly pushing for more features, lower prices, and better quality. You need to be able to respond to these demands to remain competitive.

New ideas are the lifeblood of a competitive company. When a new idea comes up, you need to be able to quickly adjust and adapt to enable the new idea. This requires agility.

Customers are looking for innovation when it comes to making a buying decision. Companies that appear innovative are more likely to get the customer's business. This means you need to respond to customer requests and customer needs quickly. Failing to do this will not only cause you to lose customers, but will also cause you to lose your credibility in the industry.

Agility is essential to maintaining a thriving business.

Security vulnerabilities

Your competitors aren't the only ones innovating. Bad actors are innovative as well.

Never before has the IT infrastructure of our valuable applications been at such great risk to security vulnerabilities and the actions of bad actors as it is today. Bad actors are not only growing in numbers; they are growing in sophistication as well. Bad actors are just as creative at coming up with new ways to attack your application as your competitors are at coming up with new ways to attack your business success.

Bad actors are constantly innovating, improving their attack vectors, and exposing the vulnerabilities of our applications.

As a company and the owner of your application, you must constantly innovate as well, to keep your applications safe and secure. You have to constantly strive to keep one step ahead of the bad actors, and this too requires agility.

Summary

Hence, the IT complexity dilemma. IT agility is critical to building a successful company, yet that very success itself adds technical debt and complexity, and this complexity leads to either rigidity or fragility. An organization that falls prey to either of these will be outpaced by its competitors in terms of innovation, and ultimately it will die. To be successful in the long term, a company must manage the IT complexity dilemma.

2

Auditing and Assessing Your IT Ecosystem

How do you avoid the IT complexity dilemma? First things first: to deal with complexity in your application or your IT organization, you need to understand where it comes from.

The first step in understanding complexity is to perform an audit of your application, your teams, your delivery and operations processes, your IT organization, and your company as a whole, to determine what parts of your system contribute to your excess complexity.

Auditing Versus Assessment

Auditing and assessment are two distinct terms that are often used somewhat interchangeably to describe the process of understanding the components that make up a complex system, such as an enterprise application. But what's the difference between the two?

Auditing is typically defined as the process of creating a *controlled inventory*. In this context, the word *controlled* implies governance. For example:

- A bank can count its money, but it has its records formally reviewed by an independent agency for accuracy when it undergoes an *audit*.

- A company keeps its own financial records, but if it is about to be acquired or undergo a merger, its records are *audited* independently to ensure they are accurate.

- If you live in the United States, you keep track of your personal finances and you submit records to the Internal Revenue Service every year to specify how much income tax you owe. Occasionally, the IRS *audits* individuals to validate that the information they are providing is correct and accurate. Other nations have similar processes.

In an IT audit, we are talking about determining, formally or informally, the components of our applications, the infrastructure they are running on, and the systems and processes they utilize.

Large enterprises may invest hundreds of thousands of dollars in such an audit, often hiring an outside auditing firm, and the process might take six months or more. Alternatively, an architect might create a quick diagram in Visio, print it out, and put it in a logbook. Both are essentially audits, but the former is much more formal than the latter.

Assessment is what happens next. Once you know what components make up your systems and applications, you perform an assessment to understand how they work together, what each component is used for, why it exists, how it's important, and the overall impact it has on the system as a whole. Often, this is part of the audit, but it doesn't have to be. Assessing often implies grading, scoring, or evaluating. For example:

- A teacher creates a test as an *assessment* to see whether their students understand the material they were taught.
- A coach evaluates how an athlete performs to *assess* how they can utilize the athlete in a team setting.
- A voter *assesses* the pros and cons of each side of an issue before casting their vote.

Auditing and assessing are complementary processes that can be employed together to determine and evaluate the makeup of a large, complex enterprise application infrastructure.

When applied to IT applications, auditing and assessing are more akin to a *survey*. A survey is a measurement tool that provides a view of the structure and architecture of a system, and that is built and maintained outside the system. It gives us an indication of how our application, infrastructure, business, or system operates and how it's structured.

What Do You Measure?

In business, including application development and IT infrastructure, our measurements are built around people, processes, and technology:

People

> Do we have the right skill sets in the right places to allow our business to function successfully? Are our employees engaged and satisfied? Are we utilizing our people most effectively?

Processes

> Do we make good and timely decisions using the right data? Are our business processes efficient and effective? Do we use our time or resources inappropriately?

Technology

> Do we have the right technologies for our business to function optimally? Are those technologies running in the right infrastructure? Are we properly utilizing all aspects of our infrastructure? Do we waste technology we have purchased by not using it effectively? Are we inefficient because we have not acquired a piece of technology that could help us?

Determining what to assess is important but highly case dependent. Focusing on questions like those shown here is a good way to brainstorm what to measure. This gives you a great perspective on what to look at when conducting your survey.

Why Do You Measure?

You can't track how your organization progresses in its growth without understanding the state of the organization and how it's currently functioning. To determine where you can improve, you must measure where you are currently.

To determine where you can improve, you must measure where you are currently.

MEASURE-TRY-MEASURE-REFINE

Before you make any change to how a system operates, you need to determine how that change might affect the system. In order to do that, you need to measure the system's current state. Then, after making the change, you can measure again and assess the impact. This allows you to refine your attempt and measure again. The result is a loop, called the *Measure-Try-Measure-Refine* loop, illustrated in Figure 2-1.

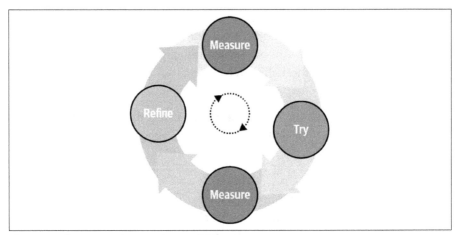

Figure 2-1. The Measure-Try-Measure-Refine loop

This is a basic process of cyclic improvement, and it goes by many other names. It's very similar to the Plan-Do-Check-Act (PDCA) or Plan-Do-Study-Act (PDSA) cycle, otherwise known as the Deming cycle (*https://oreil.ly/L6Z3h*).

In this version, we start at the top with the *Measure* step. We measure our system to understand its current state before making any changes.

We then move on to the *Try* step. Here, we attempt a change to see whether it will positively or negatively impact our system. Does it help us or hurt us?

> *You can't tell if you've improved unless you know your situation before and after every change you make.*

To answer that question, we then do another round of *Measure*. We measure our system again and compare the current state with the original state to see how it has changed. This allows us to determine whether what we tried improved our situation or made it worse.

We then *Refine* our attempt to account for the problems or expand on the benefits. The net result should be that we are in an improved situation.

This leads us back to the top, where the cycle begins all over again: Measure-Try-Measure-Refine, then repeat. This is the process of continuous improvement.

The key point is that we must measure before and after we make any change and determine the difference between the two measurements in order to evaluate the impact of our attempt. You can't tell if you've improved unless you know your situation before and after every change you make.

THE BENEFITS OF MEASUREMENT

Every change has a cost associated with it. Those costs may be tangible (engineering costs, testing costs, the operational impact of a change, etc.) or intangible (e.g., opportunity costs). Sometimes we make a change that improves our situation, but the cost outweighs the value of the improvement. We may have made a *localized improvement,* but overall we are not better off because the cost was too great. Only by measuring can we understand the real value of the change we made, as well as the associated cost.

Another benefit of measurement is that it lets you know when you're done. The cycle could go on forever, but sooner or later the improvements you are able to make will no longer be worth the cost of making them. As Figure 2-2 illustrates, measurements will tell you when to stop: when you have reached your goal, or when you have made as many improvements as you can without incurring unreasonable costs or burdens.

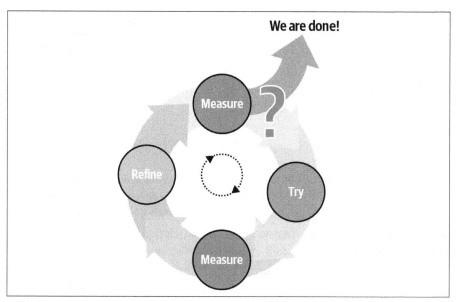

Figure 2-2. Measure to determine when it's time to stop

In summary, measurement helps us:

- Determine our current system's state and where we are in our process so we know where to focus our energies to improve.
- Analyze our changes to see whether they've made things better or worse, or improved things enough to justify the cost of the change.
- Determine when it is time to stop attempting to make improvements.

How Deep Do You Measure?

Earlier I gave the example of a large enterprise spending six months on a large, formal system audit. This is a form of measurement. It will give a complete view of the state of the system that is accurate and highly detailed—but as depicted in Figure 2-3, it will show the system state as it was six months ago, when the audit started.

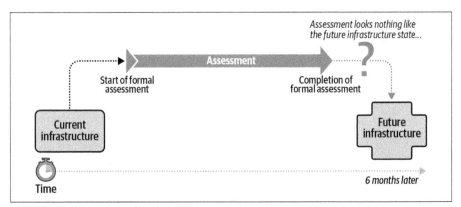

Figure 2-3. A formal assessment is inaccurate the moment it's completed

Such an audit is not of any use to us in managing systemic improvements, when we are trying to incrementally improve between each measurement cycle. If we can only make small changes every six months at the end of a formal audit/measurement cycle, then we can't make changes very quickly, and our entire Measure-Try-Measure-Refine process fails. In order to confront the IT complexity dilemma, we need to break out of these long, unwieldy, and expensive evaluation cycles. The duration of our Measure-Try-Measure-Refine loop should be measured in days or hours, not in months or years.

So, when you create an inventory of your system, when you conduct a review of your applications, when you *measure* the current state of your application and its infrastructure, how deep should you measure the system?

One viewpoint says that you need to have a deep and detailed view into your application and its infrastructure. You need to know about every CPU, data memory chip, network segment, cable, application procedure, service, node, etc. If you don't know everything, you know nothing. This viewpoint is what leads to the six-month formal external audits we talked about previously. Requiring precise measurement of everything means you can't possibly know everything you need to know in a timely manner. It can also lead to knowledge without understanding: by the time you have measured everything, you have no context for applying the understanding you've gained.

The Perfect Answer, but Too Late

I was big into computers as a kid, and living in the Midwest where storms (thunderstorms, tornados, and snowstorms) were a big deal, this generated an interest in meteorology. In the 1970s, neither of these technology fields (computers or meteorology) were very advanced. Computers were simple and just starting to be understood, and meteorology was just starting to leverage computers and satellite technology in a serious way.

Someone who was an expert in meteorology told me, "We now have the ability to completely understand what the weather will be in any given location 24 hours in advance." At the time, this was an amazing thing to hear. Meteorology wasn't anywhere near that precise back in those days, yet this person was saying we could predict the weather!

"But," the expert went on to say, "the problem is, it'll take our fastest computers three days to figure out what tomorrow's weather will be." It's not very useful to figure out what tomorrow's weather will be if it takes three days to figure it out.

This was my first lesson in understanding that too much data can be worse than not enough data.

Too much data isn't always helpful, especially if the cost of getting that data makes the data inherently less useful. If it takes you six months to collect the data, you can't use that data to determine what changes you need to make *today* to make things better *tomorrow*.

Instead, you will need to compromise. You'll need to collect some subset of the data, with the expectation that the subset you collect gives you the insight you need to extrapolate the rest of the data. Figure 2-4 illustrates this.

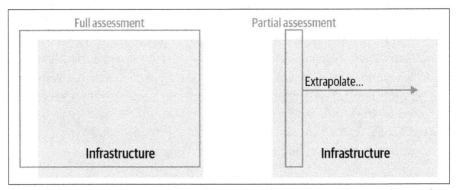

Figure 2-4. Rather than doing a full assessment, you can do a partial assessment and extrapolate the results

But what data do you need? Let's assume you have a large system that is running many large applications and you want to do an inventory that lets you know how many infrastructure components are needed by each application. You are doing this so you can compare these numbers to the amount of inventory you actually have on hand and understand whether you have excess capacity or are running your services too lean. Taking a complete inventory would be too expensive and take too long—but how can you determine what you have without doing a full inventory of the entire system? Let's look at some possibilities.

Option 1: Look at only some attributes of the inventory (such as compute) and ignore others (such as networking or storage).

One option is to look at only a subset of your infrastructure. For example, you might look only at the CPUs. How many CPUs do you have? How powerful are they? How much raw computation power does that represent? You can then determine how much computation power you have assigned to each of the parts of each of your applications.

In focusing only on raw computation power, you're ignoring other important aspects of the infrastructure an application requires, such as memory, storage, and network resources. The extrapolation you make is that if one application has twice the compute resources as another, you can assume it also has twice the networking, memory, and storage resources.

However, this assumption is rarely accurate. Just because an application has twice as many CPUs assigned to it as another, or has CPUs that are twice as powerful, does not mean that those CPUs have twice as much memory, or twice as much database storage, or twice as much networking capacity.

Using one type of resource as a proxy for your entire system inventory leads to inaccurate data and bad expectations.

Option 2: Look at a single application or service in its entirety, and ignore all other applications/services.

Another approach you can take when creating your inventory is to look at a subset of your applications or services. For example, you might decide to investigate a single application in its entirety. You determine how much computation it requires, and how much memory, storage, networking capacity, etc. You figure out what services compose this application, and what external services the application requires to operate. You make a complete inventory of everything required to run this one particular application.

Then you make the assumption that all the other applications or services in your system will have a similar set of requirements, based on some point of comparison. For example, if your analyzed application needs 25 servers and another application needs 50 servers, you can assume that the other application uses twice as much *everything* as your analyzed application.

This is perhaps a bit more accurate than option 1, but as you can imagine, it is still inaccurate. How much infrastructure a given application or service requires does not have much bearing on how much another application or service requires. Any two applications will likely look very different internally, and may use a very different mix of support services. You are still no closer to understanding the complete infrastructure needs for your entire system.

So, if neither of these options is a very useful model for getting a complete picture of the inventory needs of your system, how can you do that, short of performing a full, multimonth audit of your entire infrastructure?

The options considered here attempted to speed up the inventory process by pulling out a subset of important data from the dataset and extrapolating from that. But as we saw, this resulted in inaccuracies. Instead, how about simply spending less time creating the inventory list in the first place? Rather than trying to accurately and completely create an inventory of a small section of your infrastructure, you can create a general overview inventory that may not be very accurate, but will represent your entire system. I refer to this as an *adaptive assessment*.

Adaptive Assessment

Let's accept the fact that this may not initially be a very accurate inventory. Instead, as time goes on and you adjust your system, you'll add more data to your existing (incomplete and inaccurate) inventory, improving it little by little. That is, with each change, you'll *adapt* your inventory, adding more data to it and making it a slightly more accurate overall assessment of your system.

In the adaptive assessment, you are trading some amount of inaccuracy for speed. In other words, you are exchanging granularity of assessment for development speed.

With the adaptive assessment approach, rather than striving for perfection in complete inventory (which will take too long) or part of the inventory (which will be unrepresentative), we *estimate* the inventory of the entire system. Then, over time, we refine the estimate and make it more and more accurate.

It's an iterative approach to inventory assessment. Figure 2-5 illustrates this process. In the adaptive assessment, you are trading some amount of inaccuracy for speed. In other words, you are exchanging *granularity of assessment* for development speed.

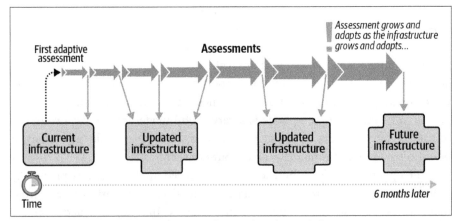

Figure 2-5. An adaptive assessment grows and expands with your infrastructure

Realizing your inventory will be worthless if it takes six months to finish (because the inventory you have six months from now will not be the same inventory that you have now), you instead create a shallow assessment of your inventory and refine it over time. As a result, you will have a much more relevant and useful inventory for a greater period of time. You will make your initial, albeit inaccurate, inventory assessment very quickly, then refine it and add more detail to it as your system changes. Little by little, it will become more accurate. Because the inventory didn't take much time to create in the first place, it will remain a more accurate representation of your *current state* than of an outdated *historical state*.

THE VALUE OF AN ADAPTIVE ASSESSMENT

The true value of an adaptive assessment is time. We will begin to talk about adaptive organizations in the next chapter, but briefly, an organization with an adaptive architecture requires decision-making cycles measured in days or weeks at most. In many cases, the action execution cycles are measured in minutes or days. Since a formal audit can take weeks or months to complete, it's useless to an adaptive organization, and wasteful. Waiting six months for the results of a formal audit is just not practical, and even if you could wait that long, the result would be a view of your systems that is six months out of date and useless. If you make daily decisions and changes, the assessment will be woefully outdated months before you ever see it.

An adaptive assessment gives you *some* actionable information immediately. Even if you don't have full access to everything that would be available in a formal audit, what you do have available to you is available at the right time. Some data when you actually need it is infinitely better than complete data when it's too late to be useful.

The key is to keep the end goal in mind. Ultimately you do want to end up with as accurate an assessment as possible, both in terms of the quality of the information and the accuracy of the information at the present time (i.e., an inventory that represents the current state of the system, not some point-in-time view of the system in the past).

> *Some data when you actually need it is infinitely better than complete data when it's too late to be useful.*

The question, then, is this: how do you decide what level of granularity you are willing to sacrifice in your assessment in order to have the data you need in a timely manner? Put another way, how granular must the data be to be useful, and when do you need it?

CREATING AN ADAPTIVE ASSESSMENT

We start with this optimistic goal: we want everything.

But we need to temper that goal with a reality check: we are willing to accept errors in what we collect. We may end up with guesses and estimates in much of our assessment in order to get our results more quickly.

We will be using the error bar approach to create our adaptive assessment. This approach results in a complete assessment—a complete inventory of our system—but that assessment is based on guesses and estimates, which may be wrong. Hence, they have "error bars." Our long-term goal is to revise our estimates as we gain more information to reduce the size of the error bars, ultimately creating a more accurate assessment, as shown on the righthand side of Figure 2-5. Our short-term goal is to create a complete inventory, with errors, quickly. This is opposed to the extrapolation approach, which strives for a partial inventory quickly, or the formal audit, which strives for a complete inventory, without errors, after a long time.

A classic error bar approach starts with colloquial knowledge about the system. "I believe we have 48 network access ports in our primary service rack." Close enough; we'll use that number for our inventory for now. At some point in the future we can verify the number: if we find it's 50 instead of 48, we can adjust our assessment, making it more accurate. But in the meantime, we have a workable number we can deal with. Knowing that we have around 48 ports in our rack is infinitely more useful than not having any idea how many there are and needing to wait several months to have an accurate count.

Adaptive assessments say, "I value being educated sooner rather than later, and I understand I will get more educated as time goes on."

DECISIONS BASED ON ADAPTIVE ASSESSMENTS

We will be using our assessments to make decisions, but it's important to understand that those assessments are not absolute. They are estimates, and will be adjusted and refined over time. Our data—our assessment—is *agile*.

As a result, the decisions we make using this data need to be agile as well. We need to be willing to rethink and reimplement past decisions when we are presented with more accurate and refined data. However, this does not mean we can flip-flop on decisions routinely.

Decision flexibility is a struggle for many IT organizations. Some organizations cannot change direction easily, even when faced with clear and compelling evidence that they are headed in the wrong direction. Meanwhile, other organizations can't stay focused on anything and constantly move back and forth in a series of nondecisions. Neither is a good place to be.

To use adaptive assessments effectively, you need to be willing and able to make decisions that stick, but also be willing to rethink those decisions when and if the refined data you have available suggests a change.

Your data has error bars, so your decisions must have error bars too. Flexibility is important, while still making actionable decisions.

The most important skill you need as an organization is adaptivity. Your architectures need to be adaptive, not overly robust. An architecture that is rigid and resistant to change is not an architecture that is suitable for adaptive assessment.

> *Your data has error bars, so your decisions must have error bars too.*

LOOSE COUPLING

Many architectural patterns support adaptive assessments, but one of the most valuable patterns you should embrace in all your architectural decisions—application, infrastructure, business—is the pattern of loose coupling.

In a loosely coupled architecture, the connection between any two modules within the architecture is as loose and flexible as possible. This concept applies to application architectures (such as service-oriented architectures), infrastructure architectures (such as cloud-centric architectures), and business and organizational architectures:

- In the case of *application architectures*, loose coupling means you must create solid APIs and contractual agreements between software services that define the expected interactions between the services. The APIs define and manage inter-service expectations, but they do not put any requirements on the actual methods, systems, and architectures used in the internal implementation of the services themselves.

- In the case of *infrastructure architectures*, loose coupling means you should depend on using infrastructure services, such as cloud-based services, that have predefined expectations about how they work. However, the user of these services does not need knowledge of how the infrastructure service itself is actually constructed or how it functions.

- In the case of *organizational architectures*, loose coupling means defining the ownership and responsibilities of individual teams independently from the ownership and responsibilities of other teams or the organization as a whole. Teams have clearly defined goals that are achievable independently, without requiring undue intervention from neighboring or interfacing teams.

In my book *Architecting for Scale* (O'Reilly), you can read much more about loose coupling. The book lays out five tenets for building highly scalable applications and organizations, several of which describe patterns that involve loose coupling. Tenet 2 is about loosely coupled applications (service-oriented architectures). Tenet 5 is about loosely coupled infrastructures (cloud-based architectures). Tenet 3 talks about loosely coupled organizations and processes. And Tenet 4 talks about risk management, which is an important part of building and using adaptive architectures.

Examples of Adaptive Assessments

There are many ways to perform adaptive assessments. How do you get started? Here are a couple of examples that apply to IT infrastructure assessments.

EXAMPLE 1: THE BRAINSTORMING ADAPTIVE ASSESSMENT

An adaptive assessment can start with nothing more than a group brainstorm aimed at identifying the parts of your infrastructure and how they work together. The result may not be very accurate at all, but it is still a useful assessment of your system because it gives you a view of how people *think* the system is constructed. As you find mistakes and correct errors, you'll grow that understanding and you'll be able to refine your team's internal understanding of how the system *actually* functions. You should encourage your team to update the assessment every time they interact with the system and make changes so that the assessment continues to improve over time.

Your brainstorming session is an adaptive assessment because it meets the two core requirements:

Generates results quickly
> It generates results at some level of quality very quickly. After the initial brainstorming meeting, you have an assessment. It may not be accurate yet, but it's a start and has immediate value.

Improves over time
> The results improve as time goes on. As your team keeps updating the assessment as they make changes, the assessment keeps improving.

EXAMPLE 2: THE CLOUD TAGGING ADAPTIVE ASSESSMENT

When using cloud architectures, a convenient way to start an assessment of your operational infrastructure is to virtually tag individual components of your infrastructure. This is particularly useful in cloud-based systems, as most cloud providers give you the tools necessary to tag individual infrastructure components. As you begin tagging infrastructure components with specific attributes, you'll start to see how you are utilizing your cloud infrastructure. You can tag infrastructure components to show which applications use a specific component, what teams are responsible for managing it, who is responsible for paying for it, and who to contact to determine when the component is being used, or whether the component is still being used at all.

Once you've done some tagging of your cloud infrastructure resources, you can generate reports based on those tags to find out all sorts of useful things, like who owns which components, what teams use which services, who uses excessive resources, who has spare resources, and who is running their resources too hot.

By putting policies into place requiring all new cloud components to be properly tagged and encouraging teams interacting with existing cloud components to add tags if they don't have them yet, you'll keep improving your assessment of how your cloud infrastructure is working over time.

Eventually, you may even want to utilize a cloud service that will enforce tagging rules. Some enterprises set up policies that ensure tagging by simply systemically deleting resources that are not tagged correctly. Nothing will encourage a team to make sure their cloud infrastructure resources are properly tagged more than having a critical infrastructure component simply disappear from their application because it wasn't tagged properly!

Your cloud tagging assessment is an adaptive assessment because it meets the two core requirements:

Generates results quickly

It generates results at some level of quality very quickly. Simply tagging a few very visible resources will give you some level of reporting ability.

Improves over time

The results improve as time goes on. Every time you create a new cloud resource going forward, make sure to tag it appropriately (software can actually require this task before it creates the resource). Existing untagged resources are tagged as they are noticed. Over time, a greater percentage of resources will be properly tagged.

The Survey Analogy

At the beginning of this chapter, I suggested that *surveying* is a better description of what we are doing than *auditing* or *assessing*, which are the traditionally used terms. The process of an adaptive assessment is more accurately described as a survey from another perspective as well.

Think about using surveys as a way to get information about people. Politicians conduct surveys all the time. Companies with visible brand loyalty use surveys to understand the value of their brand. Employers use surveys too; for example, conducting employee satisfaction surveys to determine how their employees are doing.

Let's think about such a survey for a minute. When we conduct an employee satisfaction survey, we get a list of the percentages of respondents who gave specific answers to the included questions. That's all. We then attempt to *deduce* whether our employees are happy or not from the answers. This is an assumption based on the data, not a true and complete reflection of employee happiness.

As time goes on, we can repeat the survey. We can even fine-tune some of the questions to get better and more accurate results. By comparing the results over time, we can get a more accurate picture of whether our employees are happy or not, as well as whether the things we are doing are improving employee happiness.

These surveys are non-IT examples of adaptive assessments.

Summary

An adaptive assessment is a fast and effective way to conduct an audit or assessment of your business, processes, applications, and infrastructure. It assumes that *some data, even if not 100% accurate, is better than no data at all*. A successful adaptive assessment is characterized by (1) generating quick results and (2) improving the quality of those results over time.

3

Moving to an Adaptive Architecture

One of the greatest advancements that the modern cloud era has brought us is the development and growth of the adaptive architecture. An adaptive architecture helps IT organizations build applications and systems that are more flexible and hence more agile. When used properly, this is the leading component in decreasing IT infrastructure costs associated with cloud computing. Finally, and perhaps most importantly, adaptive architectures are an important tool for reducing IT complexity and hence technical debt.

But what is an adaptive architecture?

Adaptive Architectures

An adaptive architecture is any architecture design that is able to be changed dynamically and programmatically without the need for physical intervention or manual operations.

One of the greatest tools that the modern cloud era has brought us is the development and growth of the adaptive architecture.

The left side of Figure 3-1 shows a traditional architecture. Human operators manually interact with the individual infrastructure components—servers, switches, network cables, and so on—and make the changes required to adapt to the organization's evolving needs. If additional server resources are needed, someone physically goes in and adds a new server to the rack, wires it up, and gets it up and running. This process could take days, weeks, or even months in some cases. In contrast, in an adaptive architecture such as that offered by a cloud computing provider (shown on the right in Figure 3-1), a software program determines the application's needs and dynamically, in real time, changes the IT infrastructure allocated to that application and adjusts its configuration. This is all done automatically, without human interference. If a new server is needed, one is allocated by the cloud service provider and attached automatically at the correct location within the infrastructure. Modifications that took hours or days to implement with a traditional architecture take minutes or seconds with an adaptive architecture. This allows applications' architectures to be constantly and creatively modified on the fly to meet their ever-changing needs.

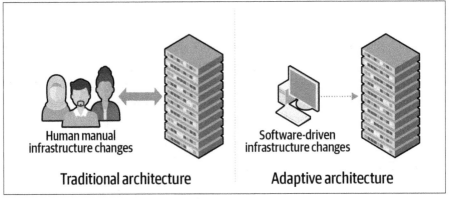

Figure 3-1. Traditional versus adaptive architecture

If a service is getting additional traffic and needs additional resources to handle that traffic, those resources can be automatically and dynamically added as needed, then freed when traffic volume drops. Need to perform a long, complex operation, such as calculating a monthly report or processing a new dataset? With an adaptive architecture you can temporarily allocate the additional resources, configure them as necessary, perform the work, then release them.

Want to try out a new idea in your running application? Allocate the resources you need and test it: if it works, you can put the resources into the IT infrastructure set, and if it doesn't, you can delete them and they go away.

Want to see how your new feature will perform under a heavy production load before launching it in production? Spin up some servers to run the feature and some servers to generate fake traffic, and give it a try. When you're done, simply delete the unneeded resources.

Need to reroute traffic around a compromised system? Launch a replacement patch and pull the compromised component out of the infrastructure. Try doing that quickly with a traditional architecture.

Adaptive Architectures in Action

Adaptive architectures give us flexibility and adaptivity. They allow us to try new ideas easily, add new resources to handle unexpected loads, and replace broken, failed, or vulnerable components quickly.

How do adaptive architectures fit into the modern application architecture? There are several places where they can assist.

AUTOSCALING

The resource needs of most modern online applications are not constant. Typically, they vary in relationship to usage, whether that's measured in terms of the number of simultaneous users, the amount of processing going on for each user, or the amount of data being handled by each user. In general, the more an application is being used, the more resources it takes to operate that application. This is illustrated generically in Figure 3-2.

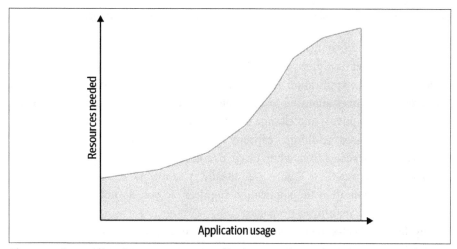

Figure 3-2. Resource requirements go up as application usage increases

In traditional application architectures, this creates a quandary. Resources need to be allocated to the application, but how many resources do you allocate? Given that historically (before the cloud), resource allocation was expensive and time-consuming, the resource allocations tended to be static. Because resource usage is dynamic, that resulted in cases where either excess resource capacity sat idle for long periods of time, or the application ran out of resources due to insufficient capacity. Figure 3-3 illustrates this.

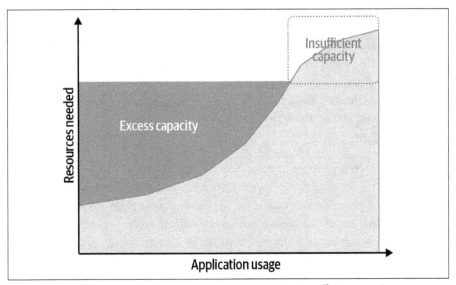

Figure 3-3. Static resource allocation results in excess capacity or insufficient capacity

If resources are statically allocated, they do not change as application usage changes. This means either you have idle excess capacity, or you have insufficient capacity and your application is starved. However, with adaptive architectures, the level of resources allocated to an application does not have to be static. It can be dynamic—adaptive—and change based on the application's needs. As application usage increases, additional capacity can be added to meet those needs, and resources can be scaled back when usage decreases.

This is illustrated in Figure 3-4. Ideally, you always have just a bit more resources available than the application requires, so you do not have significant excess capacity or insufficient capacity.

By far the best-known example of adaptive architecture is the *autoscaling* architecture. Autoscaling is a cloud mechanism that monitors the resource requirements of an application and automatically adds or removes resources to meet those needs. For example, AWS has an Auto Scaling service that can dynamically change the number of servers in a server pool: it monitors various metrics to determine whether more or less capacity is required, and either adds or removes servers to meet the existing needs.

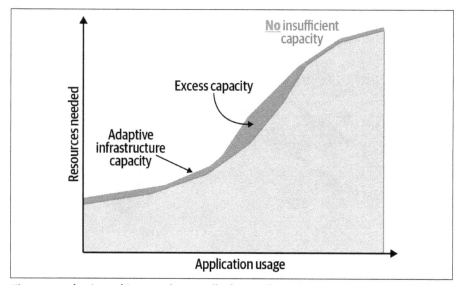

Figure 3-4. Adaptive architectures dynamically change allocated resources based on application needs

Some cloud-based services handle the allocation automatically behind the scenes. For example, AWS Elastic Load Balancer will dynamically change the size and number of servers allocated to a given application to handle the rate of incoming requests. As the number of requests increases, additional capacity is automatically added. That capacity is removed when the number of requests decreases. All of this is done completely transparently to consumers; it's handled internally by AWS's control systems.

SELF-HEALING

Imagine an application running on a pool of servers. What happens if one of the servers in the pool begins to fail or becomes damaged? This scenario is illustrated in Figure 3-5.

In a traditional, noncloud setting, the application will begin to operate sluggishly or may start failing intermittently. A human will need to get involved, log in to the failing server, and repair whatever is going wrong with it. If processes have terminated, they will need to be restarted. If a file is corrupted, it will have to be repaired. These fixes may be made quickly, or they may be time-consuming to make. If they're time-consuming, the server may be removed from the pool temporarily while the repairs are performed, causing the application to operate at reduced capacity.

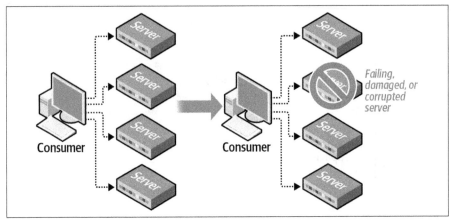

Figure 3-5. A server begins to fail in a server pool for an application

In a cloud-centric application, adaptive architecture technology can be used to assist with the repair process. If a server begins to go bad, rather than summoning a human to attempt to repair it, the failing server can be automatically terminated and removed from the pool. The adaptive architecture technology will realize that additional resources are needed in the pool and will spin up a new server and add it to the pool automatically. Figure 3-6 illustrates this.

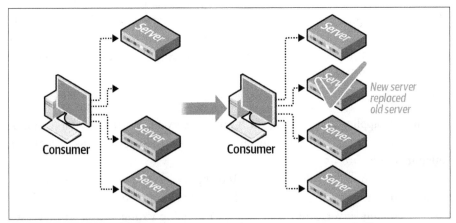

Figure 3-6. Adaptive architecture can spin up a replacement server automatically

Rather than engaging a human to attempt to repair the ailing server, the server is simply abandoned algorithmically, and a replacement server is automatically put into place.

There are two main advantages to this approach:

- A human did not need to respond to the event. The problem was fixed automatically and dynamically.

- Since a human did not have to respond and fix the problem, the issue was resolved much more quickly, and potentially with less disruption to the users of the application.

Adaptive architectures can deal effectively with many high-profile and high-impact failure modes, swapping out failing infrastructure quickly and efficiently without human intervention.

INFRASTRUCTURE AS CODE

On-premises infrastructure is traditionally constructed by racking servers and other hardware together, connecting cables, and wiring up communications components.

This is a painstakingly manual process that is not only error-prone, but also unreproducible and untraceable. It's unreproducible because of human involvement. There is no guarantee that one person will connect a computer in exactly the same manner as someone else does, and the inevitable result is a mixture of systems that are not consistent. Further, if a mistake is made and a problem is introduced, often it's not easy to trace where that problem was introduced and hence how to solve it.

Adaptive architectures provide solutions to these problems. Since your infrastructure is constructed programmatically rather than manually in an adaptive architecture, you can create standard processes and systems to consistently and repeatedly perform the same connections.

This ability has led to a best practice for infrastructure creation known as *Infrastructure as Code* (IaC). IaC is an approach to automation that allows a description of the desired infrastructure setup to be created in a simple text document using a standard infrastructure description language. This document is then fed into an IaC system that issues the appropriate calls to the cloud and component APIs to construct a real cloud infrastructure that matches the documented infrastructure. This is illustrated in Figure 3-7.

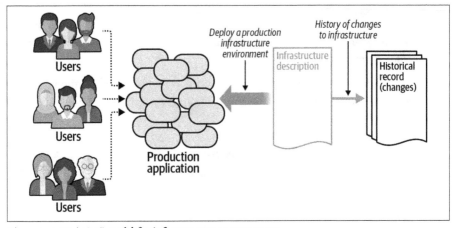

Figure 3-7. Basic IaC model for infrastructure management

Then, if a change is needed to the infrastructure, you simply make an adjustment to the document and feed it into the IaC system again, which will issue the necessary API calls to adjust the infrastructure to match the updated documentation.

There are many advantages to this model of infrastructure management. First, it simplifies the design of complex infrastructures and makes the process more approachable for the average software developer. This allows the development team to be more heavily involved in the construction and management of the infrastructure that operates their software, allowing more consistent and efficient use of hardware resources, and enables better coordination of operations and development using DevOps principles.

Second, infrastructure documents can be managed just like software code, by putting the documents into a revision control system such as Git. This allows infrastructure documentation to go through review and approval processes, just like the software application itself. In fact, the exact same processes for software quality control can be used for infrastructure quality control.

Finally, if an infrastructure change causes a problem in the operating application, a review of the revision history can be instrumental in understanding where the problem originated and determining how to resolve it. This removes the troublesome issue of trying to figure out "what changed on the server?!?" All changes are explicitly tracked and managed, and can be reviewed as needed later.

DEVELOPING IN A PRODUCTION-LIKE ENVIRONMENT

Infrastructure as Code also gives you additional benefits. Since the infrastructure document describes an accurate view of the exact hardware setup required to build your production infrastructure, that same document can be used to easily set up auxiliary, nonproduction versions of the infrastructure. This includes setting up staging and QA environments, and ensuring they are identical in design to the production infrastructure.

One benefit of this is that the common problem of divergence and infrastructure drift that often occurs between production and staging/testing environments is eliminated because all environments are created from the same source. Additionally, a developer who wants to try out a new design can easily spin up a production-like environment of their own that allows them to test their changes safely and in isolation both from production and from other developers and testers. This is illustrated in Figure 3-8.

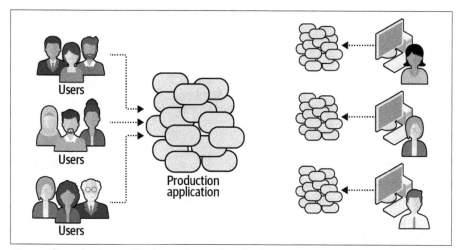

Figure 3-8. Production application and equivalent development instances can all be identical and managed

Many identical copies of the production environment (perhaps identical, or perhaps scaled down in size but otherwise identical) can be created and managed easily using adaptive architectures and IaC techniques.

LOAD TESTING

The same IaC techniques can be used with adaptive architectures to create simulated environments for load testing. Take a look at Figure 3-9.

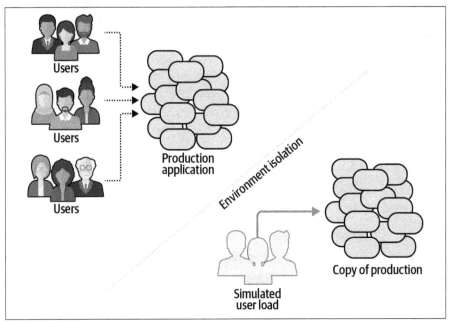

Figure 3-9. Load testing using simulated users on a copy of production

The top left shows a production application with real users, and at the lower right is an exact copy of the production setup to work with a simulated user load. This environment allows you to test various user load scenarios on an equivalent of the production environment. The testing is independent and done in complete isolation from the existing production environment, yet it provides very accurate results because the two environments are virtually identical.

Adaptive architectures allow setting up many different testing scenarios without impacting existing production environments.

Cost of Adaptive Architecture in Increased Complexity

Adaptive architectures are, on the surface, more complex than nonadaptive architectures. The increased flexibility and agility allows you to be more flexible and agile. The ability to modify your infrastructure programmatically means you can make it as complex as you want it to be. Unless managed appropriately, flexibility breeds complexity.

As we saw in Chapter 1, increased complexity increases technical debt and decreases the reliability and availability of your application. More complexity leads to fragility (instability of the application) or rigidity (resistance to making changes to the application). So, unless properly managed, adaptive architectures can lead to increased fragility or increased rigidity; neither is good.

Adaptive architectures provide you with all the great advantages discussed previously, but it's important to be aware of this potential pitfall. How do you avoid complexity while leveraging the benefits of an adaptive architecture?

Unless managed appropriately, flexibility breeds complexity.

Interestingly, you reduce complexity in adaptive architectures using the same techniques you use to reduce general software complexity in large software applications.

This means leveraging common best practices that help reduce the cognitive load when dealing with large application systems. Examples of these include:

You reduce complexity in adaptive architectures using the same techniques you use to reduce complexity in large software applications.

Modularization

Breaking software down into smaller modules, such as services and microservices, is a great way to compartmentalize complexity and, hence, reduce the amount of complexity you need to keep in mind at any given point in time.

Similar techniques work in adaptive architectures: modularizing your infrastructure and managing the modules individually reduces the impact of complexity in your application infrastructure.

For example, when architecting the frontend load balancer for an application, you can treat the application architecture itself like a black box. Similarly, when focusing on creating a dynamic infrastructure for an application using multiple services, you can treat the database high availability strategy you require as a black box, ignoring the details until later.

Loose coupling

Reducing tight dependencies between software services creates separation that reduces friction in large-scale application development. Similarly, in adaptive architectures, reducing the coupling between architectural modules lowers the complexity. By decreasing the required interaction between infrastructure components, you reduce the complexity of those components.

For example, the interaction between a frontend request cache and an application service should be restricted to basic HTTP caching protocols. There should be no deeper integration between the cache and the application. While it might seem wise to build a backdoor cache invalidation system connecting the application to the cache, avoid that in lieu of the basic cache invalidation commands included in the standard HTTP protocol.

Reuse

Reusing software components is a classic model to reduce software system complexity, and the same technique works with adaptive architectures. By using common, reusable infrastructure modules repeatedly in different places in your architecture, you can reduce complexity by increasing modularity and promoting loose coupling.

For example, if every server you deploy has the same basic structure and components, you'll have fewer variations to worry about. If each service is structured identically (or using one of a few different infrastructure structures), you can reuse the same patterns in multiple services. Similarly, using one or two standard inter-service communication models reduces the complexity introduced by each service picking its own communication protocol. Allowing individual services to control the software installed and the directory structure of the underlying servers may ease some tasks for those services, but it increases the number of moving parts for the architecture as a whole. Reuse reduces complexity.

Standardization

Restricting choices by standardizing on specific components also reduces complexity, often improving agility and time to value. For example, AWS has hundreds of different variations of sizes and shapes of servers to choose from when creating an adaptive architecture. Any of those hundreds of variations can be used in the same application. However, limiting the allowed list of choices to a select few that cover the needs of your application reduces complexity substantially.

Besides leveraging best practices such as these, there are other strategies you can employ: encouraging and enforcing consistency, repeatability, and regularity will help to reduce architectural complexity.

Example: Reducing Complexity with Tiered Security

Let's look at an example of managing and reducing complexity in an adaptive architecture. In this example, we're going to look at a cloud-based security model and see how you can use some of the techniques just described to reduce the complexity in the security setup.

Figure 3-10 shows a simplified security model for an enterprise. This enterprise has four applications that are spread across four different geographic sites. Sites 1 and 2 host applications 1, 2, and 3. Site 3 hosts applications 2, 3, and 4. Site 4 hosts applications 1, 2, and 4.

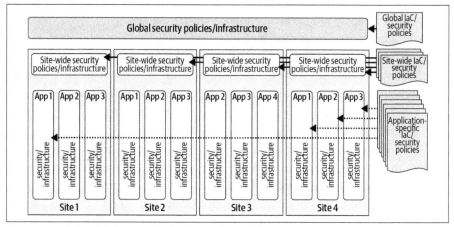

Figure 3-10. A simplified enterprise-tiered security model

There are security policies and security infrastructure requirements for every application segment at every site, plus each site has its own security requirements. This means 16 distinct and dynamically changing security requirements must be managed. If they are each managed independently, keeping track of all these requirements will be nearly impossible, especially as the number of servers, sites, and applications grows. In a reasonably sized enterprise, there might be tens of thousands of distinct security and infrastructure requirements for each component in the system.

Obviously, it would be best if all the policies and infrastructure were the same, so that there is only a single policy to track. Realistically, however, this isn't going to be the case; different locales have different security requirements, as do different applications. The complexity grows exponentially as the number of sites and applications grows.

The solution is to implement a *tiered* or *hierarchical* security model, using the modularization, loose coupling, and reuse best practices described earlier. With this model, you have a set of standard, global security policies and infrastructure requirements that apply to all applications in all locales. Next, a set of site-wide security policies and infrastructure requirements are established at the site/locale level. Finally, a set of application-specific policies are defined at the third level.

General policies and standardized infrastructure requirements are included at the top (global) policy level. These apply to everything, at all sites. The site-wide/locale-specific policies only contain policy exceptions, indicating how they deviate from the global policy. Then, at the application-specific level, the policy exceptions that apply to a particular application are defined.

You start by defining your global security policies. The goal is to put as many requirements as possible into these. Everything that applies company-wide should be specified once, at the top level—this includes things like user password requirements, security rules to keep bots at bay, edge firewall requirements, etc. These policies and requirements are applied universally across all sites and all applications.

Next, you define your site-wide policies. These should only contain exceptions to the global policies that apply at a given locale. For example, sites in the European Union that must follow the EU's General Data Protection Regulation (GDPR) requirements would have these exceptions described in their locale policies, or you might have to define different policies for sites that are in Azure regions as opposed to AWS regions. The end result is that you have a set of policies that are, mostly, described and implemented once (globally), but can be adjusted and modified as needed for a given locale. These site-wide policies can depend on and thus ignore certain rules specified in the global policies; for example, they don't have to deal with bots because the global tier deals with them.

Finally, application-specific exceptions are described at the application-specific policy level. These policies might include requirements such as which network ports the application needs, what type of traffic is expected, and scaling requirements. Policies in this layer can ignore anything established by the site-wide and global policies that applies to them, and only focus on specifying the exceptions that are unique to this application.

As many policy and infrastructure requirements as possible should be specified at the global level, with fewer and fewer requirements as you move down the tiers to the finer-grained, application-level policies. These should specify as few requirements as possible.

The net result is that, rather than tens of thousands of distinct security policies, you have three tiers, with only the required detailed exceptions at the lowest level. The vast majority of the requirements are specified once, at the global level.

The approach described here greatly reduces the complexity of managing a completely agile security model, by implementing defined processes and procedures. It uses *modularization* with the three tiers of control; *loose coupling*, since the layers are independent of each other as much as possible; *reuse* of higher-level policies to reduce the variations; and overall a *standardized model* that impacts how and where changes can be made.

There is nothing magic about this tiered model, but models such as this can dramatically simplify the development and operation of applications that employ adaptive architecture techniques.

Often, policies in a model like this are implemented in an out-of-band management tier that handles the code, configuration management, infrastructure and policy rules, and analytics in a general fashion, keeping those requirements global yet safely isolated from the three production tiers. This tier is independent of the other three and provides management and control for all the other tiers.

Summary

Adaptive architectures are a fantastic tool to facilitate the creation and operation of large, modern applications. However, used inappropriately, adaptive architectures can increase application complexity, leading to fragility and rigidity in your organization's thinking, processes, and designs. Using the same established best practices that have been used reliably in building large-scale software applications, we can leverage adaptive architectures yet manage the increased complexity, allowing us to gain the advantages they offer without the risk.

All of this means more agility, which means you can build more secure applications while enabling competitive business innovation.

4

Managing Knowledge

Knowledge management is the process of coordinating and managing the information required to maintain and operate your applications, including configuration, secrets, and documentation. Effective knowledge management involves making sure this information is in as uniform and consistent a format as possible, available as needed to everyone responsible. Knowledge management is also about reducing the amount of knowledge individuals need to operate and maintain a system. It helps ensure that everyone at the organization—from new employees to seasoned practitioners—is as productive as possible.

Understanding and maintaining complex systems tends to require a significant diversity of knowledge and expertise. The more complex a system is, the more knowledge is required to maintain it. Furthermore, the cost and difficulty of building and maintaining a system are directly proportional to the knowledge required to build and maintain it. Figure 4-1 shows this relationship.

Generally speaking, the more knowledge a system requires, the harder it is to maintain that knowledge and the more complex the system is.

Understanding a system whose operation and maintenance require diverse expertise also involves a high cognitive load. Cognitive load is a measure of the amount of information someone can hold in their working memory at one time. The more unique the knowledge requirements are, the more context you must keep within your mind in order to understand them, and hence the greater that load. Knowledge management helps reduce cognitive load, making building and operating the system more efficient.

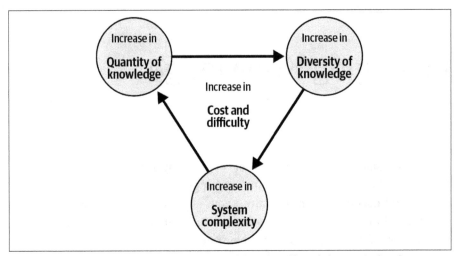

Figure 4-1. The interrelation between quantity and diversity of knowledge required and system complexity

Knowledge Variability: Choice Versus Complexity

A dichotomy exists. The more choices you give your teams in how they can build, develop, and maintain an application, the more innovative they can be. This typically results in faster time to market, more competitive products, and ultimately more satisfied staff.

The very characteristics that bring you market value and success in the short term result in increased cognitive load, technical debt, and complexity in the long term.

But this increased diversity introduces complexity, which means a greater amount of knowledge is required to understand how the system operates.

As a result, the very characteristics that bring you market value and success in the short term—specifically, innovation and flexibility—result in increased cognitive load, technical debt, and complexity in the long term. Figure 4-2 illustrates this.

The more diversity and innovation allowed in the early application development process, the greater the likelihood of market success and the more value you bring to the market. But those same qualities also increase long-term cognitive load and application complexity, adversely impacting performance and profitability.

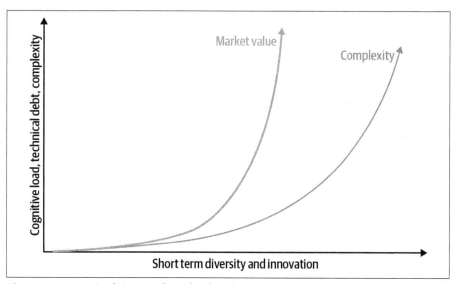

Figure 4-2. Innovation brings market value, but also complexity

Have you ever decided to implement a quick and dirty feature because you needed to get it to market quickly, despite the additional complexity and technical debt it brings to your application in the long term? This is innovation at work, introducing short-term value at the cost of long-term complexity.

Effectively managing knowledge is fundamental to reducing complexity in a system, which is required to reduce cognitive load and ultimately improve maintainability. Long-term knowledge management is often at odds with innovation and choice, and the balance must be managed to create both short-term and long-term value.

When innovating and making short-term decisions, you must factor into your deliberations the long-term cognitive effects of those choices. Innovation at all costs is a recipe for long-term disaster, but managed innovation can help create a long-lasting product offering.

The intent here isn't to say that innovation is bad. On the contrary, innovation and diversity in thought and process are critical to the success of an application (and a business). However, it's important to be aware of the sometimes-hidden long-term costs and risks associated with this mindset.

That is, when innovating and making short-term decisions, you must factor into your deliberations the long-term cognitive effects of those choices. Innovation at all costs is a recipe for long-term disaster, but managed innovation can help create a long-lasting product offering.

Managing Knowledge Requirements

The goal of knowledge management is to gather together all the available information about the tools, systems, processes, procedures, and requirements that are part of the system and that keep it operating efficiently, without overcorrecting and being overly restrictive, which can stifle innovation.

How do you control the knowledge that a system requires? Interestingly, by using the same tools, techniques, and processes you use to manage overall technical complexity in a system:

Understanding (measuring)

You can't manage the knowledge requirements of a system until you understand the breadth and scope of knowledge required to operate it.

Loose coupling

Keeping systems independent from each other—reducing the dependencies between them—decreases knowledge requirements. Dependency management, side effects, and unexpected outcomes are all problems associated with highly dependent systems. Independent systems avoid these complexities and require less knowledge to operate than highly interdependent systems do.

Standardization

Using standardized methods, procedures, and processes provides a structure to create reusable components that can be leveraged in common ways. Standardization is key to keeping systems simple and cognitive load low.

Reuse

In standardized systems, the reuse of knowledge, configurations, and information (and components and infrastructure) is easier to accomplish. Leveraging commonality in systems and keeping systems consistent and regular reduces the cognitive load of understanding how an application functions. The more you make your services and systems operate similarly to other services and systems, the less variability there is—that is, the less additional knowledge is needed to use them. This lowers the cognitive load involved in dealing with complexity.

When managing complex systems, reducing the amount of knowledge required to operate them and the variability in that knowledge has various advantages. These include:

Greater productivity
Simpler systems are easier to understand, and hence allow new employees to become more efficient at using them quickly. This reduction in time to value boosts productivity.

Increased supportability and uniformity
Simpler systems relying on standardization and reuse have more supportable components and more uniform adoption of best practices. Reuse improves resilience and reliability, which improves supportability. Uniformity reduces complexity.

Centralized Configuration

A common issue with production applications is where to store and manage the configuration, setup, and other data used to operate the application. This includes things like database access credentials, third-party service activation tokens, network router and switch configuration files, firewall configurations, cache setup parameters, database configuration information, and server configuration files.

This information is often stored at the point where it's needed. For example, as shown in Figure 4-3, network devices (firewalls, switches, routers) store their configuration information within the devices themselves, the web server configuration is stored with the web server, and the database configuration is stored with the database. The credentials required to use these capabilities are stored in the application that is using the various devices and services.

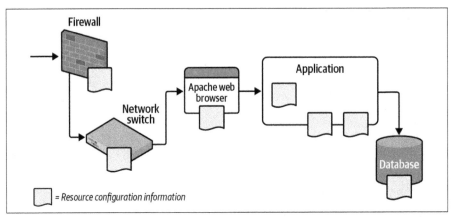

Figure 4-3. Configuration throughout an application and its infrastructure

Storing the information needed to set up and manage a service directly with the consumer of that information may seem like a good model. There are, however, several problems with this approach:

Security/vulnerability

When you store credentials with the user of those credentials, if the application becomes compromised, the referring services whose credentials you are storing also become compromised. This is bad practice from a security standpoint.

Consistency/reusability

When you store the individual configuration files in the devices themselves, there is no central knowledge of how the systems are set up and configured. This means you can't compare the configurations of, for example, one network router to another to see how they differ, or update one to match the other. In turn, this means you can't easily apply the best practices used in one configuration to another.

Availability/safety

Storing configuration files in the devices themselves also means there is no redundancy or backup of that information. If a network switch, for example, fails and needs to be replaced, how should the new switch be configured? When configuration files are stored in the devices themselves, if a device fails (or becomes compromised) and needs to be removed, the configuration is lost. If a backup is not maintained outside the device, replacing it involves the additional effort of reconstructing the require-ments for the configuration.

Traceability

> If someone changes the configuration of a needed resource, and that change ends up causing an application outage, without centralized knowl-edge it can be difficult to discover what changed recently, which means it can be difficult to find and repair the damage and mitigate the downtime. Traceability has long been recognized as valuable in software code, but it's equally important in infrastructure configuration and setup. Traceability isn't about blaming the person who caused the problem; it's about identify-ing what happened to allow the issue to be resolved more quickly, and (in the longer term) creating processes and systems to make sure the same problem doesn't occur again.

Security, reliability, consistency, and traceability are all impeded when the configuration information is stored with the resource itself—and as we saw in Chapter 1, this can have serious consequences.

The harder it is to create, update, manage, verify, or reuse an infrastructure configuration, the greater the technical debt in your application, and the greater the overall operational complexity. To combat this problem, a system for centrally managing and controlling the configurations is required.

MAINTAINING A CENTRALIZED SINGLE SOURCE OF TRUTH

The best approach to take to control and reduce the complexity associated with configuration is to maintain the configuration information centrally, outside the application and infrastructure resources themselves. This model, which relies on a *single source of truth*, protects your application's configuration and simplifies your problem diagnosis and resolution processes. Centralization of the informa-tion allows reuse and repeatability; as we have seen, this reduces complexity and improves consistency, which enhances reliability.

Figure 4-4 illustrates this approach. In centralized configuration manage-ment systems, configurations for all components are stored in a single, common location. Then, when a change is made to any of those configurations, the new version is pushed to each and every corresponding device, updating its internal copy. The authoritative versions of all configurations related to the system are stored together, off-device, and can be manipulated as a set. This centralized storage model makes it easy to track the configurations and any changes made to them. Additionally, all changes are made in a well-known location that is easier to access than the remote devices themselves.

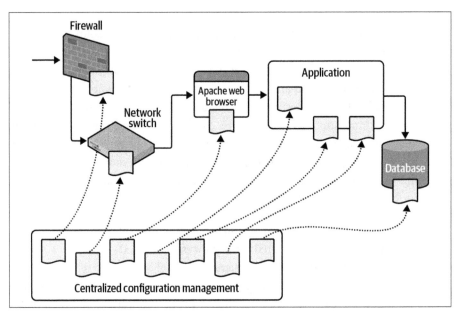

Figure 4-4. Centralized configuration management

Centralized source of truth versus single source of truth

Maintaining a single source of truth does not necessarily mean maintaining a centralized source of truth. The two concepts are different and come with different advantages and disadvantages:

- A *centralized source of truth* is where all configuration and management information is maintained in a single, centralized location.

- A *single source of truth* is where a specific piece or type of information is maintained in one location only. It can be replicated to many alternate locations (backups, different locales, etc.) and pushed to the location where it is consumed (the resource that requires the configuration), but a single copy is maintained and managed in a single location, and that is the authoritative version.

To better understand this distinction, take a look at Figure 4-5. With a single source of truth, information for a given resource is managed in a single location using a single management tool. Anyone needing to make changes to the configuration must make them in this one location. After the changes are made and have gone through any needed approval process, they are pushed to the resource(s) that require the configuration.

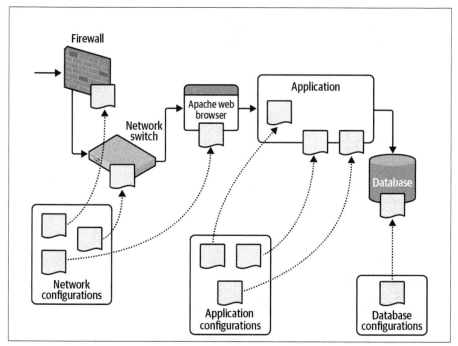

Figure 4-5. Multiple single sources of truth are decentralized

A single source of truth has the advantage of consistency and reliability. All people making changes use a consistent process for making those changes, and all changes are tracked in a single location. However, different resources can use different locations to manage their "single source." As Figure 4-5 shows, different teams (network teams, application teams, database teams) can manage their configurations independently and in different manners, while still benefiting from the advantages of those configurations coming from a single external source. That is, individual teams can store configuration files for their applications in different locations than other teams. Each configuration has a "single source," yet there is no centralized management of the configurations.

A centralized source of truth is a step beyond a single source of truth. In a centralized truth model, all configuration for the entire system is maintained in a single location using a single configuration tool. This is illustrated in Figure 4-6.

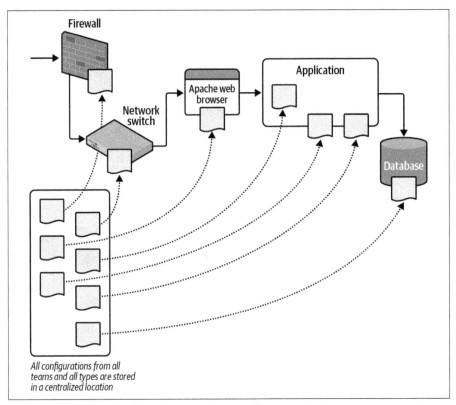

Figure 4-6. Centralized configuration across teams and resource types

Centralized truth facilitates the use of standardized best practices, reuse patterns, and layered configurations in a more consistent manner, allowing a more dramatic reduction in application complexity.

Here, the configuration for all resources is managed in one location, and all teams use the same tool to make all configuration changes for all parts of the system.

In addition to all the advantages of a single source of truth, a centralized source of truth also makes it easy to compare configurations to see how they are different: "Are the security settings of Router 123 different from those of Router 382? Why?"

Centralized truth facilitates the use of standardized best practices, reuse patterns, and layered configurations in a more consistent manner, allowing a more dramatic reduction in application complexity. While accessing a single configuration source from all parts of the application may not always be the most convenient solution, using this model more strongly encourages consistency and reuse than a simple single-source-of-truth model.

Revision management

Once the configuration is centralized, you can use revision control to manage it. Git, the tool used by software engineers worldwide to manage software source code, can just as easily be used to maintain configuration and system files. Doing so gives you all the benefits of revision management that apply to source code:

- Configurations can be backed up and maintained consistently in multiple redundant locations.

- Updated configurations can be compared to previous configurations to make sure that only the desired changes have been made and no unnecessary, undesired, or incorrect changes have accidentally been included.

- Configuration changes can be peer reviewed before they are deployed.

- Full revision control and approval workflows can be implemented to ensure that only correct and desired changes occur.

- If a decrease in performance or reliability is observed, revision history allows you to go back and see what changed at the point in time when the problem occurred, as an aid in diagnosing how to resolve the issue.

- With proper processes in place, it becomes difficult for bad actors to make configuration changes, and when they are made, the changes are easy to identify and resolve.

ARE YOU IN CONTROL?

You might be thinking that this all sounds obvious. Of course you don't store configuration information exclusively in the devices themselves. You keep backups and ensure redundancy, and you use software provided by the network resource vendors to manage your network resources. This is best practice, right?

Well, you still might be more exposed than you think. For example, do you maintain off-site copies and single-source-of-truth versions of the following configuration files:

- Apache configuration files
- */etc/hosts* files on your Linux servers
- */etc/sysconfig/network-scripts/** network scripts on Linux servers
- AWS IAM policies for the thousands of AWS components you use
- Tuning variables for your cloud-hosted MySQL database

You might be surprised by the breadth, scope, and interdependence of configuration information your complex application requires. Understanding where all your configuration requirements exist and how best to centralize them will require a complete audit and assessment of your application—the type of audit and assessment we discussed in Chapter 2. Once you have done this assessment, you'll understand where your configuration-based knowledge is stored, and you can create a strategy to manage it in a centralized single source of truth.

Reuse

Centralized knowledge management facilitates reuse. How so? Suppose all your configuration files for your applications, devices, services, and components are in one location. In that case, you can easily leverage information from one configuration in another, perhaps for a similar device. Reuse reduces reinvention, making it less likely that multiple distinct solutions to the same problem are employed. This limits variability in design and hence decreases the amount of information needed to understand how the system as a whole is operating, reducing complexity and cognitive load.

There are multiple patterns for implementing reuse, each with a distinct set of advantages and disadvantages. I will focus on two of them here.

PATTERN 1: COPY/PASTE REUSE

With the copy/paste reuse model, a system, infrastructure, or security engineer or architect looking for a configuration or design pattern to accomplish a particular task searches through the pool of existing systems for an implementation of a design pattern that appears to fit their needs. They copy the design pattern into their own system, make any adjustments as needed, and they're done! They've leveraged an existing configuration to create a new configuration, relying on reuse to make sure the new component is configured as similarly as possible to the existing component.

Advantages: Copy/paste reuse reduces the time it takes to create new configurations by leveraging known, working configurations. In addition to reducing time to completion, this approach reduces errors in the initial implementation by reusing a working implementation.

Disadvantages: Once the configuration has been copied, it no longer tracks changes in the original configuration. The new configuration and the old configuration can drift apart over time, and eventually may no longer be similar. This tends to cause complexity to increase little by little as time passes.

PATTERN 2: LAYERED/TEMPLATE REUSE

With the layered reuse model, rather than copying a configuration from one component to another, you create a shared layer of configuration that is common between the two. This *configuration template* is shared by both components. If a change is later made to that template, it propagates down and is automatically included in all configurations based on the shared layer, keeping them consistent.

Advantages: This has all the advantages of the copy/paste reuse model but eliminates the risk of slow divergence and increasing complexity over time, keeping the different configurations in sync with each other.

Disadvantages: More work is required both to create the shared layers/templates and to set up the necessary automation to use them in any given configuration, including syncing the changes automatically. Additionally, layered reuse introduces a danger: since a shared template is used in many places, a change to it for a given purpose may have unknown and undesired side effects in other places. Change management, change versioning, version pinning, continuous integration/continuous delivery (CI/CD) tooling, and change reviews can help mitigate this issue and ultimately create an environment where there is substantially less complexity because there is significantly more commonality and reuse among similar configurations.

Example: Router Configuration Files

A good example of the power of centrally managed configuration and reuse is the management of network router configurations.

A network router is used to route traffic from one spot in a network to another. Which traffic it allows to pass through can vary because of built-in firewalls, security profiles, network shaping, and routing and redirection rules. Additionally, where traffic is routed may change based on the type of traffic and the desired destination. Each of these routers has a configuration that dictates what rules the device must follow in how it routes traffic. Managing these rules can be extremely complicated, especially in a large enterprise that may have hundreds, thousands, or even tens of thousands of routers, switches, and other networking infrastructure components, all working together to create a safe, functional, secure environment for applications to operate in.

When a network has only a few of these routers, they can be managed by simply updating the configuration on the routers themselves. Most low-end routers even have web-based setup pages that allow an engineer to update the router's configuration on the fly; your home network probably has at least one networking device (perhaps a WiFi router) that offers such a configuration option.

Figure 4-7 shows an example of a router with an internal configuration. This router is configured via a web browser or API calls, and as you can see, network engineers in various locations can update the configuration as needed.

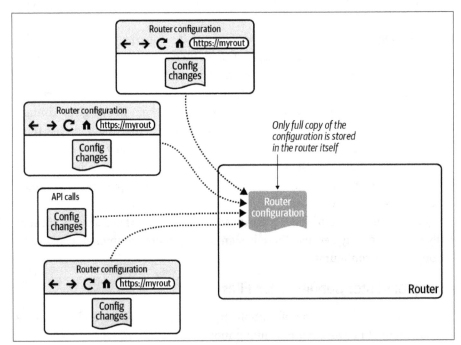

Figure 4-7. Multiple people using multiple methods to update the router's configuration

When several people are working independently on the same configuration, the changes often collide or conflict with one another. One person might make a change that causes another person's changes to fail. The result is an unstable router, which leads to an unstable network. Additionally, if that router breaks and has to be replaced, the replacement won't have the same configuration, and hence all the knowledge and expertise that went into creating the configuration in the first place will be lost. Furthermore, in an enterprise setting this router won't be alone in the network, and it will need to work with perhaps hundreds or thousands of other routers. Following this approach, each of these routers will have a distinct and independent configuration that has been hand-tailored by many different people. As time goes on, the configurations of all these devices become more and more customized, more and more specialized. Because they are each unique, the complexity of the system as a whole is very high—all because of how these routers' configuration files are managed.

Now take a look at Figure 4-8. Here, the web page and API calls that were used to configure the router have been disabled, and configuration via these means is not allowed. Instead, a copy of the configuration is stored off-device, in some centralized location. Every engineer who needs to make changes to the router's configuration makes their changes to that off-device copy. Once those changes have been approved, the off-device copy is pushed or deployed to the router in order to make them go live. The only allowed way to make a change to the router's configuration is to modify the off-device copy, then deploy it to the device, and a history of these changes can be preserved.

This model has many advantages:

- All changes people make are centralized and can be examined by all interested parties before they are deployed to the router. This reduces the likelihood that a change made by one engineer will have a negative or unforeseen effect on the changes made by another engineer.

- Each change can be logged in a revision control system so that changes can be tracked. If a network problem occurs, the history of modifications can be easily reviewed to try to determine which change may have caused the problem. The change can even be rolled back if necessary and the router restored to a previously good state until the problem can be fully investigated.

- Changes can go through a test and review cycle before they are deployed to the live production router. This may even include pushing to a staging router to verify the updated configuration works as expected before deploying it to the production network.

- Since all configurations are in a central location, they are available for inspection and review. This encourages reuse, reducing overall complexity.

- Pushing the changes to production requires some form of CI/CD pipeline. This means the process of using shared layers and templates can be automated easily.

- If a router fails, it can be replaced with a new one and an up-to-date configuration file can be pushed to the replacement router instantly, immediately getting it into the same state as the old router. This simplifies hardware maintenance operations.

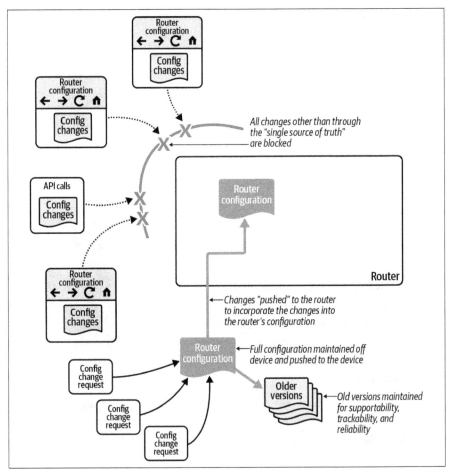

Figure 4-8. In a centralized configuration model, changes are made off-device and pushed to the device

Using centrally managed configurations reduces the overall complexity in the system, improving reliability, accountability, network availability, and, ultimately, application and company success.

Summary

Simplifying knowledge requirements and knowledge management is an important part of reducing system complexity and cognitive load. Maintaining centralized configurations is one strategy to improve knowledge management; in addition to all the benefits just described, it boosts confidence when making changes and limits the business risk involved in managing your application.

But knowledge management is about much more than centralizing configuration files. It's about providing methods to reduce the amount and diversity of knowledge about the system that is required to maintain and operate it, and about promoting reuse, simplification, and standardization, without jeopardizing the value of moving quickly and encouraging innovation.

Effectively managing knowledge requires finding the right balance between agility and uniformity, speed and completeness, complexity and understandability. Ultimately, knowledge management is about balancing short-term agility and long-term reliability in a complex system.

5

Creating Your Technology Investment Framework

As you manage your way through building and operating your IT infrastructure, you make decisions that impact which areas of your applications and infrastructure you invest in. The factors that influence your investment decisions are beyond the scope of this book, but it's important to be aware of their effect on the size and complexity of your overall system.

As a company is built, maintained, and grown, all the investments it makes will fit into a specific framework that will either enable the business or work against the business. The goal is to focus as much investment—money and energy—on the things that give the business the return on investment it requires, and as little as possible on the things that, while they might be necessary to operate the business, are not *strategic* to its operation.

Technology Investment Framework Categories

Technology investments vary depending on the type of organization. From a framework perspective, the investments will inevitably fall into one of three categories:

Sustaining

These investments keep your company moving. They include investing in infrastructure—such as communications technologies (email, phone), office space, and physical infrastructure—financial management and control, and human resources.

Disruptive

These investments are designed to build and grow your business. This might include developing new product ideas, building new features for existing products, or expanding existing products into new and interesting markets.

Performance

These investments are designed to make your business more efficient and productive. This might involve investing in marketing and sales, making reductions in cost of goods sold (COGS) or infrastructure costs, and optimizing processes and systems.

Often, companies' investment priorities shift depending on the organization's maturity and the business climate they are facing. In fact, a successful company understands where it is investing and updates its investments as necessary as time goes on.

Companies need to put money and effort into all of these categories, but they should *focus* on the things of greater importance. For example, consider your corporate email system. Companies invest in building this communications channel to facilitate communications among their employees, and between their employees and customers, partners, and other third parties. It's a necessary infrastructure component for a modern company to have.

But how much should you invest in the email system? Should you hire a large team of email experts to build the greatest email system ever? Or should you pay a few dollars per employee and give everyone a Gmail account? Or should the investment be somewhere in the middle?

To answer that question, I'd suggest simply considering this fundamental question: are you in the email business?

If your business is not the business of building and operating high-quality email services, why would you invest heavily in a state-of-the-art email system? Why not just pay the going rate for an existing email service, such as Office 365 or Google Corporate Mail, and let *that company* manage your email for you?

Just how important is email to you? Is it more important than your product offering, or a critical component of your product offering? Or is it just a tool for communicating between people involved in your business?

For example, are you a retail company like Dollar General that uses email to send company information to your employees and communicate with vendors? Or are you an email delivery service company like Mailchimp, where customers pay *you* to process their email for them?

In other words, what is your main business focus? Your answer dramatically impacts how much you should invest in email services—or any other services—for your company.

What is your main business focus? Your answer dramatically impacts how much you should invest in email services—or any other services—for your company.

Let's discuss a few specific examples where considering the actual focus of your business can impact the type of IT investments your company makes.

IT Investment Example: Are You in the Datacenter Business?

Joe's Hardware Store is a (fictitious) national chain of hardware stores famous for their customer service. You can buy a product at any Joe's Hardware Store and return it at any other Joe's nationwide. If one store doesn't have a product, they can quickly get it from another store and have it available for the customer to pick up within 24 hours. Joe's guarantees these capabilities by having a single, unified IT backend. This backend connects all the stores in the Joe's Hardware network using a common inventory, order processing, and customer service system. Additionally, customers can go online to get a copy of a receipt, check the status of a special order, or check on a pending service order. This is all enabled by the unified IT backend infrastructure.

Joe's manages the backend infrastructure via a datacenter located in downtown Prescott, a small town in western Wisconsin. The company chose this location because it was the childhood home of the CEO. However, it's 50 miles from any major population center, so getting people to work at the datacenter is difficult. Combined with fluctuating power availability, weather-related outages, and inaccessibility during major blizzards, it's hardly an ideal location for a datacenter, and Joe's wants to make a change.

But a change to what? What if it finds a new location for the datacenter, and moves all the people and equipment there, only to find out that it's hard to run a datacenter at *any* location? That doesn't seem to make sense.

So Joe's Hardware asks itself: "Are we in the datacenter business?"

In other words, is operating a datacenter important to the business that Joe's Hardware is in—namely, selling hardware—or is it a necessary but secondary part of doing business as a hardware store? Joe's decides that, while *having* a datacenter is critical to conducting its business in the way it does, *maintaining* and *operating* that datacenter is not mission-critical for the company's success. *Anyone* could operate the datacenter for Joe's. And by outsourcing the job of running the datacenter, Joe's will be able to focus more on the parts of the business that *are* mission-critical.

> *While* having *a datacenter is critical,* maintaining *and* operating *that datacenter is not mission-critical.*

So Joe's Hardware Store decides to close the Prescott datacenter and relocate all the services to a cloud service provider. This lets an expert in running a datacenter—a cloud service provider—handle the logistics and issues associated with operating the datacenter, and it lets Joe's Hardware deal with what it needs to do: sell hardware.

This story illustrates the importance of focus. By outsourcing the *sustaining* parts of its business model (operating the datacenter) to a third party, Joe's is able to focus more on the disruptive parts of its business model (selling hardware and providing the nationwide customer support the company is famous for). The company will still have to invest in the datacenter via cloud usage fees, but it doesn't have to focus on operating the datacenter. This reduction in cognitive load—and hence, IT complexity—helps Joe's Hardware remain competitive in its core, much more strategic initiatives.

> *Most companies don't have to be in the datacenter business.*

Most companies don't have to be in the datacenter business. For some companies, though, operating datacenters is core to their business. Take, for example, Amazon Web Services. AWS has become very proficient at building and operating datacenters. This is because the company needs to operate hundreds of thousands of them worldwide in order to manage its growing cloud service business.

A company's focus may also change over time. Dropbox is a company that initially outsourced its datacenter needs to a third party—it was an early user of Amazon S3, and it used AWS for all its IT needs. But as the company grew, and its competitive offerings grew to match, Dropbox discovered that to remain competitive it needed to provide more efficient data storage optimized for its needs, and hence, it needed to build its own datacenters. Dropbox now operates much of its infrastructure and data storage in its own datacenters, rather than using a cloud provider's generic storage solution. As the company matured, it discovered that operating a datacenter was in fact a *strategic necessity* for it to remain competitive.

The lesson of this example? Focus on the things that are strategically important to your business, and outsource those things that, while necessary, are not essential to your business's success.

IT Investment Example: Should You Be in the Logistics Business?

Amazon.com is a bookstore. At least that's what people called it when it launched in 1994. Even as late as 2005, when I joined Amazon, I remember a taxi driver asking me if that was "the bookstore up on the hill."[1]

Amazon quickly grew into a retail powerhouse, an ecommerce juggernaut. It sold products of all kinds, then shipped them to customers. For some time, Amazon was one of the largest users of UPS, FedEx, and the US Postal Service's shipping services.

Shipping costs were always a challenge for Amazon. The company worked hard to keep costs down and negotiated aggressive shipping agreements with all the major shipping companies.

But then a question came up. Why aren't we in the logistics and shipping business ourselves?

At first glance, you might say that Amazon is a retail store and shouldn't be involved in shipping—it should outsource that to the people who understand shipping. Yet, shipping is such a critical part of the business that outsourcing it would mean outsourcing a significant amount of control over the business as a whole.

So Amazon decided it needed to get into the logistics business, and built a giant logistics organization within the company. It bought freight airplanes and long-haul trucks, invested in growing its number of fulfillment centers, and eventually invested in a fleet of last-mile delivery vehicles and infrastructure. Now, many products you buy on Amazon are shipped—at least partially—through the Amazon logistics system. In some cases, the products are shipped and delivered

---

1 The "hill" was Beacon Hill, where the first major Amazon office was located, in the PacMed building overlooking downtown Seattle.

all the way to your door by an Amazon carrier. Amazon is now a major player in shipping logistics, and this has opened up new avenues of business. It has also allowed the company greater control over shipping speed, delivery routing, and cost containment. Amazon is one of the best shipping companies in the world, yet that wasn't its initial core business. It made an investment to solve a critical business problem, and as a result, a new arm of the business was formed.

Amazon even invests extensively in the way logistics are handled. Amazon Air is starting trials of drone delivery of packages to individuals' front doors, dramatically altering the package delivery model. It is *disrupting* the logistics business.

> *Just because a capability wasn't strategic to you initially, doesn't mean it might not be sometime in the future.*

Should Amazon be a logistics company? Most definitely, and it may end up being one of the best logistics companies around. While perhaps not obvious at first glance, this is a critical part of the company's core business: bringing products purchased on the internet directly to consumers.

The lesson of this example? Sometimes strategic necessity gives rise to new business opportunities and new opportunities to disrupt the status quo, leading to more new opportunities. Just because a capability wasn't strategic to you initially, doesn't mean it might not be sometime in the future.

IT Investment Example: How Can You Leverage Strength to Transform?

Uber started out as a modern alternative to the traditional paid car service and taxi service. By leveraging technology, it was able to provide car services at a rate substantially lower than its competitors, and with a greater degree of convenience.

This was a good business model, and Uber was an effective disruptor to those old-school transportation businesses. In fact, it was so successful that *Uber* became a generic term for getting a ride from one location to another: "Let's grab an Uber" is now more commonly heard than "Let's grab a taxi." Faced with this new competition, traditional car and taxi services struggled to survive. Many did not, but others did by adopting features of Uber's business model. Additionally, newcomers such as Lyft appeared and started competing with Uber on pricing, causing Uber to have to either adjust its business model or face being disrupted itself.

Despite these challenges, Uber built a solid business consisting of a huge worldwide network of independent drivers who owned and operated their own vehicles. Uber provided the logistics infrastructure that connected riders to drivers, as well as safety, security, and payment capabilities.

But Uber faced a problem when it came to expansion. You can expand a business like Uber's only so much. There are only so many new markets to enter, and only so many ways that people can use your service to get around town.

Then Uber realized that the network it had developed might be useful for a purpose other than driving people to and from various locations. It could also move *things* from one location to another location, on demand, quickly and easily. While this capability could be used for simple package delivery services, Uber had something bigger in mind. What about food? In a big city, timely delivery of food for lunches and dinners was always a struggle. A single restaurant could handle only a certain number of drivers and a certain number of orders in a very restricted delivery region, and the few restaurants that banded together and formed larger delivery services didn't have a lot of success. Outside of pizza delivery, it was hard to get good, consistent, reliable delivery of hot food from restaurants to homes and offices.

Uber realized that the network it had developed might be useful for another purpose. It could also move things from one location to another location... And so Uber Eats was born.

With its large worldwide fleet of vehicles and drivers, Uber had an opportunity to solve this problem. It could use its fleet to pick up food from restaurants and deliver it to customers, nearly as easily as picking up a rider and moving them to another location. And so Uber Eats was born. Again, this model was so successful that other companies started to offer similar services, and it got a boost when the global pandemic hit: Uber Eats and its competitors had huge success delivering meals from suddenly-takeout-only restaurants to suddenly-stuck-at-home diners.

Uber innovated by finding a new business to disrupt—one radically different from its original business. Before Uber, who would have imagined that the airport limousine and fast-food delivery businesses had so much in common?

Shifting Investments

As discussed in Chapter 1, excessive IT complexity can prevent an organization from shifting from, say, a sustaining or performance investment toward a disruptive investment due to competitive pressures. Remember the example of Xerox? Or a company might think it is investing in disruptive technologies, but find it's more invested in sustaining—keeping the wheels turning but not moving forward—as was the case with Hewlett-Packard. Or it might have successfully invested in disruptive technologies in the past, but be unable to find solid disruptive options for future investments and slip into irrelevance, as happened with Polaroid and Blockbuster Video. It might even simply shift its investments too late to be effective, losing an insurmountable amount of market share to innovative competitors, as in the case of Borders.

Whatever your situation, understanding how and where your business is investing will help you understand its driving force, which will help you assess your situation and understand the changes required in order to reduce complexity, increase agility, become more adaptive, and safely manage information. Based on this, you can determine a strategy to become more competitive and, hence, successful in your business domain.

In his book *Zone to Win* (Diversion Books), Geoffrey Moore suggests segmenting enterprises into four zones to enable them to more easily move from one business model to another using *disruptive innovations*. Moore's four zones are:

The performance zone
> This part of the enterprise focuses on its existing business, optimizing it and maximizing its return.

The productivity zone
> This part of the enterprise comprises the cost centers that enable the performance zone to succeed. Its focus is on efficiency, effectiveness, and compliance.

The incubation zone
> This part of the enterprise focuses on experimenting to discover disruptive innovations. It is separate and isolated from all other parts of the business.

The transformation zone
> This part of the enterprise focuses on enabling transformational initiatives to succeed.

The *Zone to Win* model describes these four zones and how companies can shift their focus between them at various points in their development, to alternatively enable or transform their business in order to stay competitive.

Summary

The investment framework your company uses will either enable the business or work against it. Your goal is to focus as much investment as possible on the business enablers, and as little as possible on the things that are not strategic to the operation of the business. Focusing your technology investments effectively is imperative: this will help reduce the cognitive load, technical debt, and business complexity of your applications, which in turn enables the innovation and agility that are necessary to thrive.

6

Starting the
Conversation

We've covered many topics in this book. We started by exploring the IT complexity dilemma, describing how the decisions IT teams make can impact the complexity of an application, which in turn can impact the cost and the organization's ability to be agile and take advantage of industry developments.

We then discussed how to assess your organization and your products to understand what they are composed of and how those parts work together.

Then we looked at how adaptive architectures can give you agility in making decisions when used appropriately, taking care that they do not inadvertently add complexity and fragility.

Next, we discussed managing knowledge. How can you organize the information required to keep a modern application working correctly without contributing to system complexity or increasing system vulnerability?

Finally, we talked about innovation and showed how and where your investments in your organization can affect it. Will an investment positively disrupt your business? Will it simply enable the business to keep moving forward? Will it have a positive or negative overall impact?

All of this discussion was centered on one overriding concept: how do you create and encourage organizational change to improve your application and your organization? These are the kinds of questions you need to ask: Can you modify the course of your product or company to enable increased innovation? Can you drive disruption in your industry as you move forward? What do you need to do now to prevent your organization from falling into the trap, as described in Chapter 1, of becoming either fragile or rigid over time? Figure 6-1 recalls this danger.

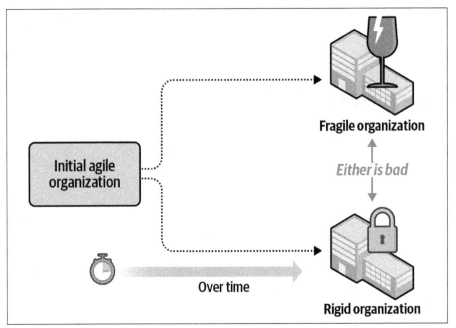

Figure 6-1. An agile organization may fail over time by becoming either rigid or fragile

To drive the desired changes in your organization and your product(s), you must start the conversation about the necessary transformation.

This may seem easier for a CEO, CFO, COO, or other CxO in your company to do than it is for you. But change does not have to start at the top. It can start at the bottom or in the middle. In fact, meaningful change, such as the type that may be required for your organization to take advantage of many of the concepts in this book, may be harder to drive from the top down or the bottom up. It may be easier to drive from the middle out.

Why is that? Because driving the sort of change you need to get the outcomes you desire for your product offerings requires a few things:

- Knowledge and expertise about the products and their position in the industry. This requires an understanding of both the code and technology of the products and what the products do for your customers and the industry at large.

- Knowledge and expertise about the customers who are using the products and/or the prospective customers your company wants to use your products.

- Knowledge and expertise about how the business is currently being operated and what changes might be needed organizationally.

This is very broad knowledge, and it's typically the type of knowledge required by an effective mid-level manager or executive. Any lower in the organization, and you likely won't have the business operational knowledge; any higher in the organization, and you'll likely lose the required connection with the product and technology details.

So, as a mid-level manager or executive, you are in fact in the perfect position to influence the types of changes described in this book.

But how do you begin the conversations? Start with a very high-level audit of the product and organization—the type of high-level adaptive assessment described in Chapter 2. Then assess how your organization is operating with respect to the structures and issues discussed in Chapter 1. How serious a complexity dilemma might you be facing? Are you deep in complexity or are you just brushing the surface? Are you already a fragile or rigid organization, or might that be in your future if you are not careful? Are you currently facing IT death or can you imagine a day when that might become a concern?

Document your findings as you go. Then, using this documentation, begin the conversation both up and down the organization. Moving down through the organization, focus on the impact of complexity and a lack of innovation. Talk about the value of adaptive architectures and knowledge management. Moving up through the organization, focus on the business costs of IT death, and how the opposing forces of complexity and agility affect how you can grow the organization. Focus on how these concepts impact the organization as a whole.

Depending on the size and complexity of your organization, these conversations may be simple or hard, and they may be well received or fall on deaf ears. But, sooner or later, they will begin to sink in, whether because they make sense to the right individuals in the organization or because some event or situation occurs that forces their recognition. Either way, this will be the moment when you can push for the changes you see as necessary to help your organization move forward.

Finally, continue to grow and learn. This book is just a starting point in your journey. Check out other books, articles, courses, and interviews by the author at leeatchison.com (*https://leeatchison.com*). Also take a look at the many other great books and courses offered by O'Reilly Media online, and the books *Cracking Complexity Now* by David Komlos and David Benjamin (Nicholas Brealey) and *It's Not Complicated* by Rick Nason (Rotman-UTP).

This is a challenge. It may appear to be an insurmountable challenge, but remember the techniques discussed in Chapter 2 for conducting an audit. You don't have to be perfect to be good. And to be good, you just need to start.

Index

A

adaptive architectures
  autoscaling and, 43-45
  decision-marking cycles, 35
  fragility, 51
  IaC (Infrastructure as Code), 47-48
  importance of, 37
  load testing and, 50
  overview, 41-42
  production-like environment, development in, 49
  resource allocation, 43
  rigidity, 51
  self-healing and, 45-47
adaptive assessment, 34
  brainstorming, 38
  cloud tagging, 39
  creating, 36
  current state, 35
  decisions and, 36-37
  error bar approach, 36
  estimated inventory, 34
  granularity of assessment, 34
  loose coupling, 37-38
  value of, 35
application architectures, loose coupling, 37

application development teams, SaaS companies, 7
architectures
  adaptive, overview, 41-42
  application architectures, 37
  autoscaling and, 43-45
  IaC (Infrastructure as Code), 47-48
  infrastructure, 37
  loading testing and, 50
  loosely coupled, 37
  organizational, 37
  production-like environment, development in, 49
  self-healing and, 45-47
assessment, 26
  (see also adaptive assessment)
auditing, 25
  controlled inventory, 25-26
Auto Scaling service (AWS), 44
autoscaling, adaptive architectures and, 43-45
AWS (Amazon Web Services) Auto Scaling service, 44
AWS Elastic Load Balancer, resource allocation, 45

B

B2C (business-to-customer), SaaS companies, 6
brainstorming adaptive assessment, 38
brittleness, 15

C

centralized configuration, knowledge management, 61-68
cloud tagging adaptive assessment, 39
cognitive load, 57
    reducing, 59
competitiveness in modern IT organizations, 22
complexity
    brittleness, 15
    choice and, 58-60
    engineers' knowledge, 16
    flexibility and, 51
    in IT organizations, 19-20
    messy desk syndrome, 17-18
    organizational pain and, 15-18
    technical debt and, 11-15
    tiered security and, 53-55
configuration, centralized, 61-68
    router configuration files, 69-73
consistency, centralized configuration and, 62
controlled inventory, 25, 26
copy/paste reuse model, 68
credential storage, 62
Cunningham, Ward, 11

D

decisions, adaptive assessment and, 36-37
Deming cycle, 28
depth of measurement, 30-33

development in production-like environment, 49
development team, 7-8
DevOps, modernization and, 9-10
disruptive innovations, 82

E

error bar approach to adaptive assessment, 36

F

flat management structure, 2
flexibility, complexity and, 51

G

GDPR (General Data Protection Regulation), 54
granularity of assessment, 34
growth inhibitors, 3

H

Hewlett-Packard, IT death and, 21
hierarchical security model, 54

I

IaC (Infrastructure as Code), 47-48
    operations teams and, 9
icing the cake, 18
infrastructure architectures, loose coupling, 37
innovation, knowledge management and, 59
    disruptive innovation, 82
inventory estimates, adaptive assessment, 34
IT complexity dilemma, 1
IT death, 20-21

IT organizations
    complexity in, 19-20
    development team, 7-8
    DevOps, 9-10
    flat management structure, 2
    mature, 21
        competitiveness, 22
        security vulnerabilities, 22
    operations team, 8-9
    software development and, 3
        non-SaaS organization, 5-6
        nonsoftware-focused organization,
            4-5
        SaaS-focused organization, 6-7
    structure, 2-10

K

knowledge management, 57
    cognitive load, 57
    configuration, centralized, 61-68
        router configuration files example,
            69-73
    innovation and, 59
    knowledge variability, 58
        cognitive load reduction, 59
    requirements management, 60-61
    reuse and
        copy/paste model, 68
        layered/template model, 69

L

layered/template reuse model, 69
load testing, adaptive architecture and, 50
localized improvement, 29
loose coupling, 52
    knowledge requirements, 60
loosely coupled architecture, 37, 38

application architectures, 37
infrastructure architectures, 37
organizational architectures, 37

M

Measure-Try-Measure-Refine loop, 27-29
measurement
    benefits, 29-30
    Deming cycle, 28
    depth, 30-33
    knowledge requirements, 60
    Measure-Try-Measure-Refine loop,
        27-29
    PDCA (Plan-Do-Check-Act), 28
    PDSA (Plan-Do-Study-Act), 28
    people, 27
    processes, 27
    technology, 27
messy desk syndrome, 17-18
modularization, 51
    tiered security and, 54

N

non-SaaS IT organization, 5-6
nonsoftware-focused IT organization, 4-5

O

OaC (Operations as Code) tools, 9
operations team, 8-9
organizational architectures, loose cou-
    pling, 37
organizational change, conversation start,
    85-88
organizational pain, complexity and, 15-18

P

PDCA (Plan-Do-Check-Act), 28

PDSA (Plan-Do-Study-Act), 28
people, measuring, 27
Polaroid, IT death and, 21
processes, measuring, 27
productivity, knowledge requirements, 61

R

redundancy, centralized configuration and, 62
resource allocation, adaptive architectures, 43
reuse, 52
   copy/paste model, 68
   layered/template model, 69
revision management, centralized configuration, 67
router configuration files, 69-73

S

SaaS (software-as-a-service)
   non-SaaS IT organizations, 5-6
   operations teams, 8
   SaaS-focused organizations, 6-7
   technical debt and, 11
security
   centralized configuration, 62
   tiered security, complexity and, 53-55
   vulnerabilities, 22
self-healing, adaptive architectures and, 45-47
shifting investments, 82-83
single source of truth, centralized configuration, 63-67
software development, 3
   non-SaaS organization, 5-6
   nonsoftware-focused organization, 4-5
   SaaS-focused organization, 6-7

standardization, 52
   knowledge requirements, 60
supportability, knowledge requirements, 61
surveys, 26, 40

T

technical debt, 2
   complexity and , 11-15
   growth, 11-14
   negative aspects, 14
   repayment, 11
   SaaS and, 11
technology investment framework
   datacenter business example, 77-79
   disruptive, 76
   logistics business example, 79-80
   performance, 76
   shifting investments, 82-83
   sustaining, 75
   technology leveraging example, 80-81
technology, measuring, 27
tiered security, complexity reduction and, 53-55
traceability, centralized configuration and, 63

U

understanding, knowledge requirements and, 60
uniformity, knowledge requirements, 61

V

variability, knowledge variability, 58-60

X

Xerox, IT death, 21

About the Author

Lee Atchison is a recognized industry thought leader in cloud computing, and the author of the best-selling book *Architecting for Scale* (O'Reilly), currently in its second edition. Lee has 36 years of industry experience, including eight years at New Relic and seven years at Amazon and AWS, where he led the creation of the company's first software download store, created AWS Elastic Beanstalk, and managed the migration of Amazon's retail platform to a new service-based architecture. Lee has consulted with leading organizations on how to modernize their application architectures and transform their organizations at scale. Lee is an industry expert and is widely quoted in publications such as *InfoWorld*, *Diginomica*, *IT Brief*, *Programmable Web*, *CIO Review*, and *DZone*. He has been a featured speaker at events across the globe from London to Sydney, Tokyo to Paris, and all over North America.

Colophon

The cover image is by Susan Thompson. The cover fonts are Guardian Sans and Gilroy. The text font is Scala Pro and the heading font is Benton Sans.

CPSIA information can be obtained
at www.ICGtesting.com
Printed in the USA
JSHW011359170423
40438JS00006B/141

9 781492 098492